Dramaturgical Analysis of Social Interaction

DRAMATURGICAL ANALYSIS OF SOCIAL INTERACTION

BY

A. Paul Hare

AND

Herbert H. Blumberg

WITH SELECTIONS FROM
THE WORKS OF

Erving Goffman

David A. Snow, Louis A. Zurcher, and Robert Peters

R. S. Perinbanayagam

Ronny E. Turner and Charles Edgley

PRAEGER

New York
Westport, Connecticut
London

Library of Congress Cataloging-in-Publication Data

Hare, A. Paul (Alexander Paul), 1923-
Dramaturgical analysis of social interaction / by A. Paul Hare and Herbert H. Blumberg.
p. cm.
"With selections from the works of Erving Goffman, David A. Snow, Louis A. Zurcher and Robert Peters, R.S. Perinbanayagam, Ronny Turner, and Charles Edgley."
Bibliography: p.
Includes indexes.
ISBN 0-275-92762-8 (alk. paper)
1. Social interaction. 2. Drama—Social aspects. I. Blumberg, Herbert H. II. Goffman, Erving. Selections. 1988. III. Title.
HM291.H1566 1988
302—dc19 87-30534

Library of Congress Catalog Card Number: 87-30534
ISBN: 0-275-92762-8

First published in 1988

Praeger Publishers, One Madison Avenue, New York, NY 10010
A division of Greenwood Press, Inc.

Printed in the United States of America

The paper used in this book complies with the Permanent Paper Standard issued by the National Information Standards Organization (Z39.48-1984).

10 9 8 7 6 5 4 3 2 1

Contents

Preface

In this volume we have collected accounts of events viewed from a dramaturgical perspective and lists of variables and hypotheses from those social scientists who have been most active in using this approach for the past forty years (Berne, 1964; Brissett and Edgley, 1975; Burke, 1945; Burns, 1972; Cochran, 1986; Goffman, 1959; Harré and Secord, 1972; Lahr and Price, 1973; Lyman and Scott, 1970, 1975; Perinbanayagam, 1985; Sarbin, in Allen and Scheibe, 1982; V. Turner, 1974). Although the history of the dramaturgical perspective goes back further than that, having its origins primarily as an off-shoot of symbolic interactionism, early proponents of this view relied more on anecdotal evidence to support their insights than on actual case studies. Some of the results of the application of the perspective in the observation of social events are presented in Part III.

As dramaturgical analysis has yet to be developed as a formal theory, our compilation of the insights both of persons who have written in this mode and those writing about the theater represents the "state of the art." However, there is still plenty of space on the theoretical stage for others to add new ideas and to show the relationships between the various sets of ideas that have already been proposed.

The reader who is interested in some of the earlier writing using a dramaturgical perspective may wish to look at four collections of material: Lahr and Price's book entitled *Life Show* (1973); Brissett and Edgley's *Life as Theater* (1975); Combs and Mansfield's *Drama in Life* (1976); and Stone and Farberman's *Social Psychology through Symbolic Interaction* (1981, second edition), which includes some articles from a dramaturgical perspective but covers a much wider field.

For *intra*personal dramaturgy see, for example, McDougall (1985) and Rowan (1983).

Works that discuss the relationship between dramaturgical analysis and related perspectives such as structuralism, social exchange, ethnomethodology, and narrative psychology include the writings of Levine (1977), Mangham and Overington (1982), Mitchell (1978), Perinbanayagam (1982a), and Sarbin (1986).

A. Paul Hare
Herbert H. Blumberg

Acknowledgments

We wish to thank those publishers who have allowed us to reprint selected material from books and journals. Specific acknowledgments are given in the text at the points where the quotations or illustrative material appear.

Jim Rowland and Christine Keeler prepared the final copies of the Figures.

We are also most grateful to colleagues who read the manuscript at various stages of preparation. In matters of both style and content their suggestions have simplified the task that the reader will face in understanding and applying the perspective of dramaturgical analysis. Thank you Gerry Stimson, Bert Kritzer, Mary Jo Deegan, Amy Kritzer, Chris Wilson, Carol Troen, and June Hare.

APH
HHB

PART I

Drama, Self, and Audience

1

The Dramaturgical Perspective

This introductory chapter on the dramaturgical pespective begins with a brief summary of the phases in the development of performance. We then review the basic concepts used by Burke, Harré and Secord, Sarbin, and others in dramaturgical analysis. Some of the basic concepts are then depicted in a diagram to illustrate the roles that are played onstage, backstage, offstage, and in the audience. A subsequent diagram summarizes some of the concepts used to describe levels of role- and self-involvement. This is followed by a discussion of the extent to which the term "drama" is being used to describe real aspects of social behavior, or whether the term is only used as a metaphor. The last section of the chapter provides an overview of the material in the book.

PHASES IN A PERFORMANCE

An instance of social interaction is a *performance*. Any performance, including a theatrical one, starts out from an *idea* about a situation and the action that will unfold within the situation. The idea may be a single *image* that has the program for action packed into it, much as a symbol in a dream may be a merger of waking events. On the other hand, the idea may be as fully developed as the detailed *script* for a play, with parts for each member of the cast and stage directions to guide the performance. A single image is more likely to guide the interaction, for a time, in a small informal group, whereas a script guides the interaction in a formal organization, such as a factory, where behavior at the work place is highly structured. There can also be ideas of intermediate complexity, such as a *theme* (including both a direction of movement and a minimum set of roles to be enacted) to guide an instance of elementary collective behavior in an acting crowd, or a *plot* (with a detailed scenario, defined roles, and an indication of the stages a group must go through to reach a goal) to guide the activities in a social movement.

Once the idea has been put forward, an *action area* is needed. This may involve building or finding an action area and making provision for an *audience*, if there is to be one. As Burke has noted in his use of the concept *scene/act ratio* (1968), all aspects of the stage or scene suggest limits for the action that will be appropriate in that setting. The stage set suggests the time, both clock time and historical time, and the mood of the play.

The next phase of the performance involves the recruitment of the *actors* who must learn their *roles*. This is followed by the *enactment* of one or more themes and, finally, after the last curtain call, a period of appraisal of the effect of the action on the *definition of the situation*, both for the actors and for the audience.

CONCEPTS USED IN DRAMATURGICAL ANALYSIS

A similar set of basic concepts has been provided by persons who have been working with a dramaturgical perspective. For example, Burke (1968:446) suggests that for any *act* (performance) there must be an *agent* (actor) and a *scene* (stage) in which the agent acts. To act in a scene, the agent must employ some means, or *agency*. Burke goes on to suggest that an act must have a *purpose*. To these five concepts, which he first introduced in 1945, he later added a sixth concept of *attitude*, as an ambiguous term for incipient action. For the present analysis, Burke's concepts of agency, purpose, and attitude are all aspects of the idea that becomes the focus of action (see Overington, 1977, for a discussion of Burke's concepts).

For Harré and Secord (1972:149–53, 176–204) dramatic performances are analyzed in terms of the *episode* as the natural unit of social activity. During a single episode the participants follow a plan or carry out the actions necessary to complete a task. The beginning and end of an episode is often marked by a ceremony.

Three types of episodes are identified: (1) formal episodes, which can be either liturgies or games, in which there are rules for what should be done, when and by whom, (2) routines, such as servicing a car, where the actions follow a natural sequence of events, and (3) entertainments, where there is neither upshot nor outcome from the actions performed. Formal episodes can in turn be classified according to eight types derived from three dichotomies: genuine–simulated, ceremonial–casual, and cooperative–competitive. For the analysis of social behavior from a dramaturgical standpoint, Harré and Secord (1972:205–206) suggest that one should "1. Treat the episode one is engaged in, whether as actor or audience, as a dramatic performance. 2. Reconstruct the script, the stage directions, etc., which can be analyzed according to the Role–rule model scheme, as if it were a play script in which rituals, games, routines and entertainments were simulated." (See also Harré, Clarke, and DeCarlo, 1985:86–87.)

Sarbin (Allen and Scheibe, 1982:19–25; or Sarbin, 1976:14–22) emphasizes the context in which the action takes place by classifying both the dramaturgical approach and the "field theory" of Lewin (1935) as instances of *contextualism*. Sarbin suggests that the root metaphor for contextualism is the historical event. The historical event consists of "an ongoing texture of multiply elaborated episodes, each leading to others, each being influenced by collateral episodes, and by the efforts of multiple actors who perform actions in order to satisfy their needs and meet their obligations." The implication is that there is constant change in the structure of situations and in the positions occupied by the actors. Sarbin grants that contextualism may at first appear chaotic to those who have been schooled in ideographic or mechanistic world views, since the dramaturgical approach assumes that there is constant change and novelty. (See also Rosnow and Georgoudi, 1986).

Sarbin lists the principal characteristics of the dramaturgical perspective as follows (Allen and Scheibe, 1982:20–21; or Sarbin, 1976:16):

1. The meaning of an event arises from social interaction.
2. The self (the recognition of individuality and of separateness of others) is constructed in social interaction.

3. Actors respond to situations but also mould and create them.
4. The unit of analysis is not the individual but interacting persons.
5. Individuals construct and reconstruct meanings to make sense of their observations.

Some of the main contributions to the dramaturgical perspective have come from persons associated with the "Chicago School" (cf. Cooley, 1902; Mead, 1934; Goffman, 1959) and have been seen as a subtype of *symbolic interactionism*. Brissett and Edgley (1975:2, 7) call attention to this fact in a book of readings entitled *Life as Theater*. They suggest that the dramaturgical perspective can be summarized in a set of characteristics that are similar to those given by Sarbin.

Lahr and Price (1973:6), in their book *Life Show: How to See Theater in Life and Life in Theater*, sum up the dramaturgical perspective by noting that "the life performer . . . is continually being placed in cultural scenes in which special performances are demanded." Additional discussions of the concepts used in dramaturgical analysis include Dewey (1969), Edgley and Turner (1975), Hopper (1981), Hughes (1976), Lipp (1984), McLeod (1984), Merelman (1969), and Perinbanayagam (1982b).

A summary of some of the basic concepts for dramaturgical analysis that have been presented so far, as well as some additional concepts, are depicted in Figure 1.1. The large rectangle represents the action area. This can be divided into two parts: *backstage* and *stage*. The backstage area is where actors prepare for their roles and where special effects are produced to influence the audience. This is where those who arrange the setting and provide props, costumes, and makeup do their work (*backstage staff*). The stage is where the action takes place in full view of the audience. For any action there may also be *offstage* areas where persons who have organized the activity (*producers*) and those who may have rehearsed the cast and are providing cues for the action (*directors*) remain hidden from the audience. In addition, there may be the person who provided the original idea or script for the performance (*playwright*). This does not complete the list, as there may also be persons who cater to the needs of the audience. Thus the basic list of roles may need to be expanded to suit particular situations.

On stage, in Figure 1.1, there are two sets of nested circles: one to represent the role played by the principal actor who is the theme

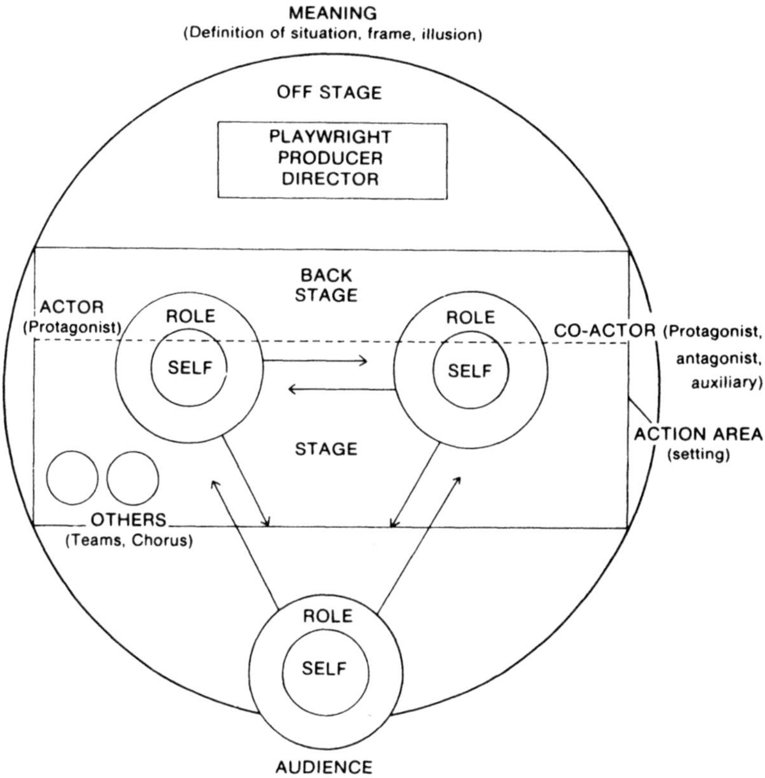

Figure 1.1
Basic concepts for dramaturgical analysis.

carrier of the moment (*protagonist*), and one to represent some co-actor (who may be a protagonist for another idea, an *antagonist* of the first idea, or an *auxiliary player* supporting the protagonist). Inside each of the larger circles representing the *roles* there is a smaller circle to represent the *self*, the individual characteristics that each person brings to the role. The smaller circles near the protagonist represent additional players who may form a *team* in support of the protagonist. One version of this type of team work is found in the activity of the *chorus* in a Greek tragedy, which underlines the mood of the protagonist. Another example would be the person who provides language translation for a speaker at an international gathering. In front of the stage a set of nested circles represents the *audience member*. Even if there is no external audience, the actors are themselves an audience for their own and others' actions. Even if no other actor or audience member is physically present, all social behavior is performed with some idea of the expectations of one or more *reference groups* in mind.

LEVELS OF ROLE AND SELF INVOLVEMENT

Moving on from Figure 1.1 to complicate the dramaturgical perspective still further, we observe with Sarbin (Allen and Scheibe, 1982:21; or Sarbin, 1976:17) that "the theater-goer, as well as the participant in any social interaction, must be able to place an arbitrary frame around a given episode or scene to separate it from other episodes or scenes." For this frame for action Burns (1972:17) uses the term "illusion." *Illusion* is only a specifically theatrical term for the process of confining attention to what is appropriate or meaningful or consequential for a defined level of reality. The *frame* signifies the degree of seriousness or playfulness that is to be attached to an event. The three *levels of reality* that are accepted in the theater also apply to everyday life. These three levels are:

1. The "pretend" reality of games, sports, parties, and ceremonies.
2. The "alternative" reality of occupational worlds and ritual.
3. The "overriding" reality concerned with the deliberate efforts to change or defend definitions of the situation or the rules of the game.

Sarbin (Allen and Scheibe, 1982:40–44; or Sarbin and Allen, 1968:492–96) provides a more detailed list of eight levels of reality. These levels Sarbin considers degrees of organismic involvement (effort) that an actor puts into a role:

Zero — Noninvolvement
I — Casual role enactment
II — Ritual acting
III — Engrossed acting
IV — Classical hypnotic role taking

V — Histrionic neurosis
VI — Ecstasy
VII — Bewitchment

Some of these eight types are more closely related to the actor's role, others to the self or *personality* of the actor. The actor seems to be quite conscious of the part being played for some, and unconscious for others. Another set of roles on the unconscious end of the continuum is the type of family game that Berne (1964:44) defines as "an ongoing series of complementary ulterior transactions progressing to a well-defined predictable outcome." A common game played between spouses is "If it weren't for you," when one of the pair complains that all sorts of things might have been accomplished if it were not for something the other had done. An indication of the way in which Burns' and Sarbin's levels of reality and Berne's "games people play" (1964) fit together is given in Figure 1.2 (Hare, 1985:153).

At the top of Figure 1.2 is a continuum for role behavior and at the bottom a continuum for self-oriented or personality-based behavior. The left end of each continuum represents behavior that is unconscious, the right end behavior that is conscious. The circle in the middle of Figure 1.2 represents the *interpersonal behavior* that we observe that is ordinarily some combination of the expectations of role modified or expanded by the tendencies of personality. However, sometimes what we see is governed almost entirely by personality, at other times almost entirely by role.

The continuum for role behavior governed primarily by role goes from the least conscious, on the left, where the role is imposed without the cooperation of the person, to the most conscious, on the right, where the person is fully alive to the possibilities of maintaining or creating a role. Most of the discussions of roles in the social psychological literature deal with the right-hand end of the continuum. This includes Burns' present, alternative, and overriding realities and Sarbin's first three levels of casual, ritual, and engrossed acting. On the unconscious end of the continuum would fall many of the "games" that Berne describes, and Sarbin's levels of classical hypnotic role-taking and bewitchment.

Sarbin's types of histrionic neurosis and ecstasy seem to have a closer relationship to personality than to social role. Thus they are

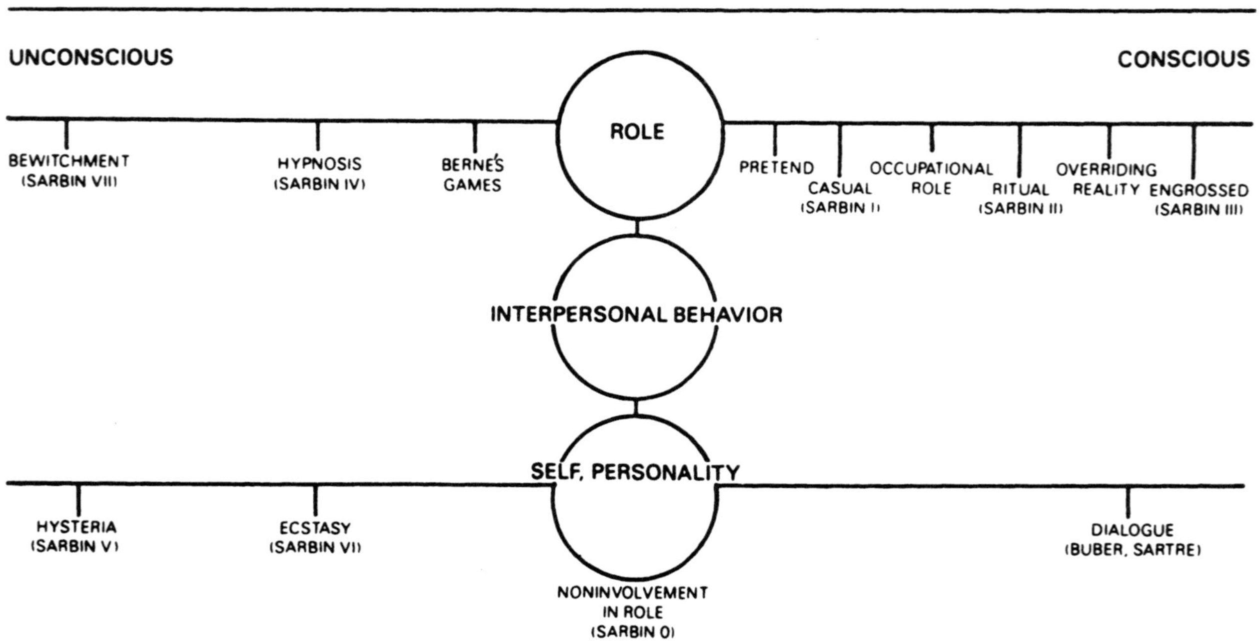

Figure 1.2
Levels of conscious role and self-involvement.

(From A. Paul Hare, *Social Interaction as Drama: Applications from Conflict Resolution*, p. 153. Copyright © 1985 by Sage Publications, Inc. Reprinted by permission of Sage Publications, Inc.)

placed on the unconscious end of the personality continuum, with histrionic neurosis probably being less of a conscious activity than ecstasy states. At the most conscious end of the personality continuum would be the highly conscious interactions between the self and the other, represented by Buber's dialogue between I and Thou (Buber, 1970) and the absence of Sartre's "Bad faith" (Caws, 1979:76). This form of interaction that appears to be "self" to "self" would seem to be the same as that identified by Moreno as the "tele" relationship (two-way empathy) (Moreno, 1972:238ff).

SOCIAL DRAMAS: REAL OR METAPHOR

One of the issues for persons who first began to do dramaturgical analysis was whether social interaction was actually a series of dramas or whether "drama" was only being used as a metaphor to illustrate the way in which social interaction seemed to take place. Some, such as Sarbin cited earlier, called attention to drama (or contextualism) as a "root metaphor" for analysis. Some argued that social interaction really was a performance. For example, Burke (1968:448) said that "drama is employed, not as a metaphor but as a fixed form that helps us discover what the implications of the term 'act' and 'person' *really are.*" McCall (Stryker, 1981:16) agreed that real life is drama. For him "identity, meaning, and social acts are the stuff of drama; as drama involves parts to be played, roles implicit in the parts must be conceived and performed in ways expressive of the role. The construction of social conduct involves roles and characters, props and supporting casts, scenes and audiences." MacCannell (1973:10) made a similar statement: "The structural principles which make what happens on the stage meaningful are the same as those which give meaning to everyday life." Some took the position that life was not essentially drama but that the dramaturgical perspective could be added to other forms of social-psychological perspectives (Goffman, 1959). Finally some took an intermediate position that on some occasions the persons involved in interaction are intent on solving a real problem, but on other occasions they are more concerned with presenting an "illusion" to an audience (Burns, 1972; Gusfield, 1981).

For the present analysis, we take the view that there is a continuum ranging from everyday activities that do not have a dramatic quality, through social events that are consciously staged, to theater productions. This continuum will be elaborated in Chapter 5 when we consider the effect of an audience on an event and whether the event is primarily real or symbolic.

A PREVIEW OF COMING ATTRACTIONS

Our book is divided into three parts. The first provides an overview of ideas about drama, self, and audience. The second part takes us through the phases of a typical dramatic production. The third part presents four examples of varieties of enactment by persons writing from a dramaturgical perspective.

In this first part, Chapter 2 includes a discussion of the four basic types of drama (tragedy,comedy, melodrama, and farce), as they appear in the literature on theater, and an analysis of Polti's 36 dramatic situations. Chapter 3 summarizes the concepts of Goffman, Harré, and others who have described in considerable detail the ways in which persons in everyday life may be preoccupied with presenting an image of themselves to others. At the same time these persons are trying to discover the true selves of the others. Chapter 4, by Goffman on teamwork, describes the way in which an individual actor may be supported by others who collude to present a common face. Chapter 5 provides an overview of descriptions of the function of the audience. The presence or absence of a formal audience determines whether the actors will be primarily concerned with presenting an idea to others or with carrying out their own activity.

Part II includes chapters on the first three phases in the development of a drama (actable idea, staging, and actors and roles) and the fifth phase (new meanings). Chapter 6 elaborates the concept of the "actable idea" with examples of ideas that fall along the continuum from a vague "image" to a detailed "script." Chapter 7, on staging, includes a discussion of the concept of "scene/act ratio," which refers to the fact that each setting implies a range of behavior that is appropriate for that setting. Edelman provides examples of political settings and Cavan of the arrangement of seating in bars. Chapter 8 gives more details concerning the basic roles found in any enactment and reviews the literature on role theory, including the concept of the "self-role merger," a discussion of role conflicts, and the action involved in entering and leaving a role. Chapter 9 considers the new meanings that may arise for actors and audience after an enactment, especially as they might occur for an individual in the process of "self-reconstitution," or in search of a new meaning for a group or for a society.

Each of the chapters in Part III, as an example of enactment (the fourth phase of drama development), illustrates the way in which the dramaturgical perspective has been applied to some area of social interaction. In Chapter 10, Snow, Zurcher, and Peters describe their field study of the celebration in a U.S. college town after the football team had won a game. Chapter 11 illustrates the ways in which the level of creativity in the actions of individuals and groups involved in a protest in South Africa and the images that the groups held of each other led to a tragic outcome. In Chapter 12, Perinbanayagam describes the theory of good and evil of the people of Jaffna, a Hindu–Tamil community in Sri Lanka, and the way in which this theory guides their ceremonies of departure and arrival. Finally, in Chapter 13, Turner and Edgley show how judicious rhetoric, behind-the-scenes preparations, flexible facilities, control of social settings, and staged impressions are orchestrated to perform a successful funeral in the United States.

SUMMARY

Any performance goes through the phases of (1) an idea (that could be in the form of an image, theme, plot, or script), (2) selection of stage, (3) recruitment of actors and training for roles, (4) the enactment, and (5) new definition of the situation for actors and audience.

Burke's concept of scene/act ratio refers to the fact that all aspects of the stage or scene suggest limits for the action that will be appropriate in that setting. In Burke's terminology the idea has three aspects: agency (means), purpose, and attitude (an ambiguous term for incipient action).

Harré and Secord classify "episodes" of social activity in three categories: formal, routines, and entertainments. For analysis they suggest that each episode be treated as a dramatic performance that is following a script.

Sarbin emphasizes the context in which the action takes place by classifying the dramaturgical approach as an instance of "contextualism." The perspective is characterized by assumptions that the meaning of both the event and the self is constructed by actors through social interaction, and that the unit of analysis is not the individual but interacting persons.

Some of the basic concepts for dramaturgical analysis can be depicted diagrammatically with a rectangle for the action area, divided into a stage where the action takes place and a backstage area where the actors prepare for their parts and where backstage staff who support the action do their work. There are offstage areas for producers, directors, and playwrights. Each actor and member of the audience is represented by two nested circles: an inner circle for the self, and an outer circle for the role being played. The interpersonal behavior is some combination of self and role. Actors' roles may include a protagonist, antagonist, and auxiliary players, some of whom may form a team to support the protagonist, as did the chorus in early Greek plays.

Sarbin and Burns suggest various levels of reality that may constitute the frame (or illusion) that gives meaning to a particular episode. These various levels of reality, together with those described by others, can be seen to fall along one of two continua—one for role behavior and one for self-oriented or personality-based behavior. Each continuum goes from behavior that is unconscious at one end to behavior that is conscious at the other.

For some writers drama is only a metaphor for the way social interaction takes place. However, for others the ideas taken from the theater describe real life as it is. In this volume it is assumed that there is a continuum ranging from everyday activities that do not have a dramatic quality, through social events that are consciously staged, to theater productions.

2

Types and Divisions of Drama

For our analysis of types and divisions of drama we introduce the four types that have been traditionally distinguished in the theater and note their application to everyday life. Each of these types is, in turn, made up of one or more dramatic situations that can be grouped in seven sets, all told. The central figures in these dramatic situations are often heroes, villains, or fools. In the second half of the chapter we will describe the ways in which social dramas are often divided into phases, acts, and scenes and show how a time line may be used to illustrate the development of a drama.

Persons who have written about staged theatrical productions distinguish different types of dramas. The categories they use—for example, tragedy and comedy—will apply most directly to those instances of social interaction that are controlled by a script. However, they also apply to less structured forms of social interaction, such as those that follow a plot, theme, or idea. Since the task of sorting out the various forms of social interaction according to the types that will be identified in this chapter remains to be done, we will only be able to give a few examples based on the summary by Hare (1985:41–45, 55).

FOUR TYPES OF DRAMA

Hamilton (1939:17) defines a play as "a representation, by actors, on a stage, before an audience, of a struggle between individual human wills, motivated by emotion rather than intellect, and expressed in terms of objective action." He notes that in the four types of plays that are usually identified in histories of drama through the nineteenth century, in two—namely, *tragedy* and *comedy*—the characters control the plot, whereas in the other two—*melodrama* and *farce*—the plot controls the characters (Hamilton, 1939:72–75). Tragedy and melodrama tend to be serious, with an unhappy ending, in contrast to comedy and farce, which have a lightness of style and a happy ending (Sobel, 1959). In the theater and in life, comic or farcical scenes may be included in tragedies or melodramas to provide some relief from the seriousness of the situation. Stebbins (1979) has noted instances in everyday life when comic relief provides momentary respite from the seriousness of or lengthy concentration on a collective task.

Bentley (1965:195–315) also discusses these four types of drama at some length, observing that comedy provides hope because it takes place on the other side of disaster; the transcending emotion is joy. Fry (1962:68) elaborates on this theme. Both tragedy and comedy deal with truth, but "comedy is an escape, not from truth but from despair: a narrow escape into faith. . . . In tragedy we suffer pain; in comedy pain is a fool, suffered gladly."

In the twentieth century, the distinctions between these four forms of stage plays and the newer forms have become increasingly blurred (Sobel, 1959:128). However, earlier dramatists seemed to have anticipated a current set of ideas in social psychology that are brought together under the label of "attribution theory" (Raven and Rubin, 1983:103–18). According to attribution theory, all outcomes are divided by ordinary people into two types, bad and good. People then attempt to find a cause to which they can attribute the outcome. The causes tend to be classified as one of two types—either some person (the self or another) or the situation. These two dichotomies provide a fourfold classification that is essentially the same as the four types of drama:

1. *Tragedy* has a bad outcome that is attributed to some person or persons.
2. *Comedy* has a good outcome, also attributed to a person or persons.
3. *Melodrama* has a bad outcome that is attributed to the situation in which the actors find themselves.
4. *Farce* has a good outcome, also dominated by the situation.

In everyday life it is perhaps easiest to identify events of a tragic nature, as when one or more persons are killed because of some "fatal flaw" in the character of a gunman who snipes at passersby in a public place. The interethnic conflicts and conflicts between protestors and police that take place in many parts of the world have a more melodramatic nature because the participants are playing out social roles, with little attention to personality differences. Persons who find themselves in embarrassing situations or are the butt of practical jokes become actors in farcical events. Finally, those occasions when people can gain enough distance on their problems to be able to laugh at them in song, cartoons, mime, or free-flowing dialogue provide the essence of comedy.

THIRTY-SIX DRAMATIC SITUATIONS

In addition to describing the four major types of drama, many writers have suggested that there may be only a limited number of plots composed of some set of *dramatic situations*. For example, Bentley (1965) listed three types of tragedy: (1) suffering and endurance, (2) destruction and renewal, and (3) sacrifice and expiation.

One of the most extensive analyses of dramatic situations was conducted by Polti in the early 1900s. His work, originally in French, was translated into English in 1921 and republished in 1977. A previous drama critic had asserted that there were only 36 basic dramatic situations. Polti sought to challenge this statement by categorizing some 1,000 stage plays and 200 other dramatic stories. At the conclusion of his work, Polti decided that there were only 36 dramatic situations, after all. However, he suggested that variations on the 36 situations could be created by altering: (1) ties of friendship or kinship, (2) the degree of consciousness or free will, (3) the energy of the acts that must result, and (4) the parts, so that a group of characters is substituted for an individual (Polti, 1977:119). He further noted that most plays are combinations of several dramatic situations: "there is no situation that may not be combined with any other, so that they develop logically, or pose a dilemma, or each pertains to a particular group or a particular role" (1977:120).

The common theme in all the situations, Polti concluded, was that every dramatic situation springs from a conflict between two principal directions of effort. At the curtain rise, one of these directions of effort persists. At the arrival of the other (innocent or responsible person), the struggle begins. One is the protagonist and the other is the antagonist. Disequilibrium arises from the introduction of a material object, circumstance, or third person, giving a "plot." Some of the additional actors play roles that support the protagonist and some the antagonist. These additional auxiliary roles include parts for choruses, confidants, crowds, clowns, and "figurants" (prophets or porters who are precursors of important persons). The same person may play many roles, and the same role may be played by many persons (1977:119–23).

Polti's work was published long before Parsons emphasized the importance of four system levels (biological, personality, social system, and culture: see Effrat, 1968) for the analysis of social behavior, and long before Bales introduced the field diagram as a method for the analysis of roles in groups (Bales and Cohen, 1979). It is now possible to consider Polti's material in the light of these newer perspectives to see whether there might be fewer than 36 basic dramatic situations.

The roles and objects described by Polti in each of the 36 dramatic situations were depicted on a field diagram displaying the location of the roles in terms of four dimensions of social interaction (Hare, 1985:24–25): upward–downward (dominant–submissive), positive–negative, serious–expressive, and conforming–anticonforming. The field diagrams were then sorted into sets according to system level and the interaction dimension that seemed to be dominant.

The results of this type of analysis (Hare, 1985:167–70) reveals that the 36 basic situations can be grouped into seven sets of dramatic situations. Four are at the social system level, where the focus is on the interplay of several roles, and three are at the individual or personality level, where the conflict is between different parts of the self. Briefly, the seven sets are as follows:

A. Social system level

1. Hero vs. villain: A hero (upward, positive, and serious) as protagonist, a villain (upward, negative, serious) as antagonist, and

a third party or object. Conformity or anticonformity is not a major issue.

2. Vanquished and victor: The emphasis is on the relative power of the protagonist (downward) and the antagonist (upward).
3. Love/hate triangle: The emphasis is on the positive–negative dimension of social interaction. Persons who should like each other do not. The situations of this type generally involve an imbalance of liking in a triangular relationship.
4. Crime and punishment: The emphasis is on the conforming–anticonforming dimension. The crime that is committed may be of any type. However, a family member or loved one is usually involved, and the anticonforming behavior is often either adultery or incest.

B. Individual or personality level
   1. The fatal flaw: The upward, positive, ideal self is contrasted with the upward negative behavior of the protagonist. This is similar to set A(1) at the social system level except that the struggle is between two aspects of the same person.
   2. Search: The theme emphasizes the upward–downward dimension as the relatively powerless protagonist searches for someone or something while overcoming obstacles.
   3. Self-sacrifice: The theme is a conflict between conformity to the ideal self versus some pragmatic action.

Klapp (1962), in his analysis of the changing American character, used an even shorter list of dramatic situations. He suggested that the central figures in social interaction consisted of *heroes, villains,* and *fools*, either alone or in some combination. He noted (1962:17) that heroes are praised, followed, set up as models, and given a central part in dramas. Villains and fools are negative models, respectively, of evil to be feared and hated, and absurdity to be ridiculed.

DRAMAS, PHASES, ACTS, AND SCENES

The *drama* is the largest unit of our analysis. Harré and Secord (1972:147–53) use the term "episode" to describe a single drama. (See also Watson and Potter, 1962.) They identify an *episode* as any natural division of social life. For our analysis we have suggested that this natural division includes the *phases* of developing an actable idea, the selection of an action area, the selection of actors and the rehearsal of their roles, and enactment of the idea, followed by a new definition of the situation (or a reinforcement of the previous definition). However, just as in the theater, there can be a play within a play or a series of nested dramas. For example, are the events surrounding the founding of a new State to be considered as a separate drama, or the last act in a drama that began with the idea of independence, or the first act in a drama of the enactment of nationalism? It could be all of these. Thus it is left for the observer to identify the beginning and ending of a natural division of social life.

Whichever unit has been selected as the drama, there may be two or more identifiable subdivisions, or *acts*, within a phase, and within the acts even smaller units or *scenes*. The characteristics of a scene in the theater, as identified by Van Laan (1970:229) are as follows:

1. Any narrative unit, having its own beginning, middle, and end.
2. Stands out in an overall pattern of action as a self-contained sequence of incidents.
3. Limitations may be a change of locale or a temporary clearing of the stage.
4. In Greek tragedy, the odes or the chorus separate the scenes.
5. There is a shift in focus.

In a real-life situation a change in scene is often marked by a change in the persons involved or a movement to a new action space—for example, shifting a conversational area from the living room to the kitchen while food is being prepared.

The larger unit, the act, may combine two or more scenes. The divisions between acts are similar to those between scenes in that a change in action area or actors is often involved, but the change is more evident and often there is a lapse of time between acts. In the theater this lapse is signaled by the lowering of the curtain. In real life there may be a break in the enactment of hours, days, or even longer periods. Many groups in society assemble only once a week or once a month. For groups of this type, each meeting usually constitutes an act, and subdivisions of the meetings, as members come and go, or the activity shifts, constitute scenes.

Although we might refer to each of the natural divisions in our drama as an act (following the convention in the theater), we will use the terms *act* and *scene* to refer to subdivisions in the enactment phase of the drama. The preenactment activities—developing an actable idea, selecting an action area, and selecting actors and rehearsing their roles—will be referred to as *phases*. The term *phase* will also be used to indicate the postenactment period when new meanings are assigned to the activity.

SEQUENCE OF PHASES IN PROTESTS IN SOUTH AFRICA

The sequence of phases that has occurred in protests in South Africa illustrates the way in which many types of activity can be subdivided into "natural units" (Hare, 1980). The eight natural units are as follows:

1. *Planning*: the period of time prior to the actual event during which the protestors select a theme and an action area and plan their roles, if the event is organized. In the case of an unorganized event the group may respond to a theme in a matter of minutes.

2. *Initial action*: the initial action of the protesters that begins the enactment phase of the drama. This action is the most important as it can set the mood for all actions that follow. In some cases the initial planned action never takes place since the protesters are intercepted on their way to the action area. In such a case, the initial action is usually a response to police action and is less likely to have the symbolic significance that the protesters had hoped for. This action constitutes Act One.

3. *Police or authorities arrive and demonstrators react*: the mere arrival of police or authorities in the action area may be enough to set off a reaction by the demonstrators, especially if the police are in full riot gear with rifles or other lethal weapons. Some or all of the protesters may disperse at this point if they think that protest is no longer possible. This is Act Two, unless as noted above the initial action is actually a response to the arrival of the police. In that case the enactment begins here.

4. *Interplay of police action and demonstrator response*: the police do not usually stand as observers, they act in some way. They may

warn the protesters not to go further, or order the crowd to disperse within three minutes, or attempt to disperse the crowd with baton charges and tear gas. This act can go on for some time if demonstrators disperse and regroup or move from place to place. This interplay, if it occurs, is Act Four.

5. *Dispersal and arrests*: eventually the police may disperse the crowd. At this point the police may divide into small groups or individually pursue suspected demonstrators down side streets and into homes. This is the point at which a "police riot" is most likely to take place, since the individual police are no longer within sight of their officers. This is the time when innocent bystanders are most likely to be beaten or shot. At this point the drama is in the hands of the police; their theme of punishment or retaliation dominates the action. The response of the protesters is to attempt to disappear into the anonymity of the black community. This is Act Five and the end of the enactment phase. The next three phases of postenactment activity relate to the "new meaning" that may be assigned to the enactment.

6. *Sweeps and interrogation*: some time after the event hundreds of riot police or other police may surround a black area, letting no one in or out. This is likely to be very early in the morning, with the police moving from house to house, demanding entry, to see whether any youthful protesters are inside.

7. *Trials*: some months after the event a few demonstrators may be brought to trial. Some are acquitted and some are convicted. In each case it is quite likely that the judge will conclude that on the basis of the evidence the police were not at fault for any injury that occurred.

8. *Private or public reports*: much later, private or public reports, in the form of books or proceedings of commissions appointed to investigate the protest, may be published that try to give a balanced picture or set the record straight. This final act is the one in which persons on both sides try to establish the "meaning" of the action. Police try to round up demonstrators and gather other evidence so that the government can make its case that "law and order" has been maintained. Those sympathetic to the demonstration try to gather evidence that the "riots" were justified and that the police response was unwarranted or a symptom of the state of repression. However defined, the event becomes a model to be emulated or avoided in further action.

TIME LINE

For the analysis of a drama of any length it is helpful to construct a *time line* to indicate pictorially the sequence of events and the major subdivisions. The time line is usually a straight line divided into hours, days, months, or whatever time units are appropriate, with marks and labels to indicate the limits of phases, acts, and scenes. If levels of creativity or any other aspect of the behavior of the actors has been recorded, the time line may also include a graph to indicate fluctuations in this activity (see example in Chapter 11, and Hare, 1976, 1980).

Marsh, Rosser, and Harré (1978:84–90) used two time lines to compare the activities of British soccer fans during home games and away games (see Figure 2.1). From observations both inside and outside the sports grounds, the observers discovered an invariant sequence of activities. The most obvious point noted by the observers was that the soccer game serves as a focus for other events that precede it and take place afterwards. For the soccer fan, the drama lasts from about 11 o'clock in the morning until 6 or later in the evening. Where traveling to away games is involved, an even longer sequence is present. By placing the time lines for a home game and an away game in the same figure, Marsh et al. present a picture of what both groups of rival fans are doing during every soccer game.

For the home team the first phase of dressing up begins about 10:30 a.m. as the fans put on their "gear," which has distinct symbolic value. The second phase involves association and assembly. In the case of home games, fans meet their friends at prearranged places and, as small groups, engage in varied but regular activities, such as meeting in a pub or "hanging around" some location. For away games the length of the preparatory phase usually depends upon the distance to be traveled. On the average, busses leave about 11 a.m., but this can vary widely. Most fans, however, arrive at the bus departure point well in advance and once more "hang around." During this period subgroups form, some sporadic chanting and singing might break out, and seats on the bus will be "booked."

The bus trip constitutes another preenactment phase, which is a kind of rehearsal of the chants and songs that will be used at the game. The next phase consists of assembly at the end of the field

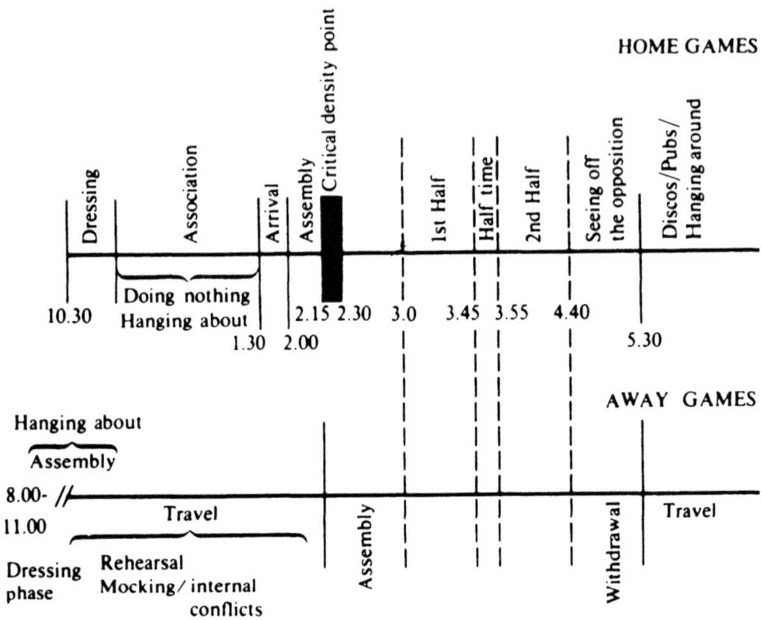

Figure 2.1
Time lines for dramas of soccer fans at home and away games.
(From Peter Marsh, Elisabeth Rosser, and Rom Harré, *The Rules of Disorder*, p. 85. Copyright © 1978 by P. Marsh, E. Rosser, and R. Harré. Reprinted by permission of Routledge & Kegan Paul.)

reserved for the fans of either the home or away team. Once the critical density of fans is reached, the enactment begins. For some fan clubs the critical density is 100 persons, for others five times that many. Each half of the game can be considered an "act," as the fans carry out their dual task of spurring their team on to victory and denigrating both the opposition team and its supporters. The interval at half time is also a separate "act" when fans may have the first opportunity to "get at" their rivals at the tea stalls. At the end of the game, the two sets of fans again have an occasion for contact with each other as they leave the grounds. For the final act, the fans of the away team return by bus and the fans of the home team take up their usual Saturday night activities of discos, pubs, or hanging around. In this case the observers do not report that the final phase includes assigning any new meaning to the activity.

SUMMARY

Following the tradition of theater, social drama can be classified as one of four basic types: tragedy and comedy, in which the characters control the plot, and melodrama and farce, in which the plot controls the characters. Tragedy and melodrama tend to be serious with an unhappy ending, in contrast to comedy and farce, which have a lightness of style and a happy ending. These four types are similar to the fourfold classification derived from attribution theory in which a good or bad outcome is attributed either to the actors or to the situation.

An analysis of Polti's 36 dramatic situations in terms of four system levels and four dimensions of interaction revealed seven sets of situations: Four were at the social system level: one containing a struggle between a hero and villain, and the other three emphasizing either relative power, love versus hate, or conforming versus anticonforming behavior. The other three sets were at the individual or personality level, dealing with the heroic or villainous characteristics of a single person, or with the relative power of the protagonist, or with self-sacrifice of an ideal for some pragmatic action.

Klapp suggested that the central figures in social interaction consist of heroes, villains, and fools, either alone or in combination.

A social drama, like a theatrical production, may have identifiable preenactment phases when the actable idea develops, the action area is chosen, and the actors are selected for their roles and rehearse. The enactment phase may be the only visible part of the performance. Often the enactment phase is divided into several natural units, or acts, and these in turn are composed of smaller units, or scenes. Changes in scene can be identified by changes in the idea, action area, or cast. Acts are set off by similar demarcations, often with longer lapses of time between them. The postenactment phase when the new meaning is established may also be less visible and occur much later than the enactment. In a typical sequence of protest and police response in South Africa, there were eight identifiable phases, from preenactment planning to postenactment publication of private and public reports.

One way to record the development of a drama is by a "time line" indicating the amount of time taken by each of the natural units of activity. As an example, time lines were used to compare the activities of British soccer fans at home and away games. For both groups of fans there are pregame phases of dressing up, assembly, and rehearsal. The enactment phase begins just before the game and continues until the home fans have "seen off" the fans of the opposition. The final phase involves returning to the usual Saturday night activities.

3

Presentation of Self

In this chapter we summarize some of the research that has represented a major focus within the dramaturgical perspective, namely a focus on the ways in which the individual presents the "self" to others. Goffman, a major contributor to this type of observation, introduced the concept of "face work" to refer to an individual's attempts to save face and avoid feeling embarrassed through some avoidance or corrective processes. As an example of impression formation we cite some of Goffman's research on the Shetland Islands. This is followed by a second example of research by Messinger on the ways in which patients in a mental hospital manage impressions to appear sane. The chapter closes with a description of a "monodrama," during which an individual plays several parts, and "altercasting," a term used to describe a situation in which an individual induces others to play supporting roles in a personal drama.

PRESENTING AN IMAGE OF THE SELF

In a staged theatrical production an actor or actress may well call upon personal experience as an aid in projecting a role that has been learned for the occasion (Mixon, 1983). Similarly, in everyday life a person may be preoccupied with presenting an image of *self* to others, thus adopting a particular "style" (Harré and Secord, 1972:215), while at the same time trying to discover the nature of the true selves of the others. Wilshire (1982a:226) puts it this way: "to be a self is to be a human body that is mimetically involved with other such bodies but nevertheless has a capacity to distinguish itself consciously from others and to regard its history and its prospects as its own."

Throughout the self presentation each individual must be able not only to act, but to direct the performance and to take the role of critic as well as the perspective of the audience (Lyman and Scott, 1975:109–10). When possible, actors will strive to associate themselves with desirable images and dissociate themselves from undesirable images (Schlenker, 1980). The teasing of each other that children do in play can be seen as a way of preparing for the maintenance of self-control in later life (Stone, 1982:203).

Goffman has written a series of books that provide insights into this process, beginning with *The Presentation of Self in Everyday Life* (1959) and continuing through a long list (1961, 1963, 1967, 1968, 1970, 1972, 1974). Most of the attention is given to microanalysis of informal encounters such as gatherings on the streets, in parks, or in restaurants. When a formal organization such as a mental hospital is observed, it is the "backstage" behavior of doctors, nurses, and patients that Goffman (1968) finds most interesting. The "strategic interaction" (calculated, gamelike aspects of mutual dealings) of secret agents and spies provides examples of ways in which persons are able to structure a course of action (Goffman, 1970:x). This type of interaction is characterized by a series of "moves"—structured courses of action that objectively alter the situation of the participants (Goffman, 1970:145). Since Goffman has contributed so much to the dramaturgical approach, his work has been the subject of a great deal of comparison and criticism. Some examples of this critique are the works of Messinger (1962), Meltzer, Petras, and Reynolds (1975:67–109), Deegan (1978), Ditton (1980), Sharron (1981), Wilshire (1982a:274–81; 1982b), and Miller (1984). Articles that apply or elaborate Goffman's perspective include Aguilar (1980), Buss and Briggs (1984), Dotter (1980), Manning (1982), Snow (1979), Watson and Potter (1962), and Wilkinson (1974).

FACE WORK

It is Goffman's view that all of the persons involved in an instance of interaction are trying to save *face*, and thus their basic approach to one another is one of distrust. Harré (1979:3) endorses this observation by asserting that "the pursuit of reputation in the eyes of others is the overriding preoccupation of human life."

Goffman identifies two kinds of *face work*—that is, of actions taken by a person to make whatever the person is doing consistent with face (1967:12–23):

1. *Avoidance processes*: the use of go-betweens (third parties), or avoiding actions or situations that would be inconsistent. If a person fails to prevent an incident, it is still possible to maintain the fiction that no threat to face has occurred. Goffman gives as an example an occasion where a person acts as if an event that contains a threatening expression has not occurred at all. The person may not by any outward sign admit that someone's stomach is rumbling or the person may not "see" that another has stumbled. In general, tactful blindness of this kind is applied only to events that, if perceived at all, could be perceived and interpreted only as threats to face.

2. *Corrective processes*: an interchange of presents or visits, or saying "excuse me" and "certainly." This is likely to occur when the participants in an undertaking or encounter fail to prevent the occurrence of an event that is expressively incompatible with the judgements of social worth that are being maintained. When an event of this kind is difficult to overlook, then the participants are likely to give it accredited status as an incident and to try to correct for its effects. The corrective interchange typically involves four moves. First, attention is called to the misconduct; second, the offender is given a chance to correct for the offense by making an offering; third, the persons to whom the offering is made can accept it; and, finally, the forgiven person conveys a sign of gratitude to those who have given the indulgence of forgiveness.

EMBARRASSMENT

Embarrassment occurs, Goffman has observed (1967:97–108), when an individual does not do what ought to be done, given the social identities of the participants and the setting. During interaction an individual is expected to possess certain attributes, capacities, and information that fit together into a self that is at once coherently unified and appropriate for the occasion.

The signs of extreme embarrassment include: blushing, fumbling, stuttering, an unusually low- or high-pitched voice, quavering speech or breaking of the voice, sweating, and other signs of nervousness. Symptoms of a subjective kind are also experienced by the individual who is embarrassed such as constriction of the diaphragm, a feeling of wobbliness, and consciousness of strained and unnatural gestures. If a person is only mildly embarrassed, these symptoms may occur, but in a less perceptable form. An individual thus flustered will make some effort to conceal the condition from others present by assuming a fixed smile, or emitting a nervous hollow laugh, or being busy with the hands, or glancing downward to conceal the expression of the eyes. The gestures provide the individual with a screen to hide behind while attempting to bring feelings and actions back to an appropriate state.

Since individuals dislike feeling or appearing embarrassed, a tactful person will avoid placing them in this position, or will often pretend not to know that they have lost their composure or have grounds for losing it, thus protecting their face and feelings and presumably making it easier for them to regain composure or at least hold on to what composure remains. If the embarrassment is too great, people may give up trying to conceal or play down the uneasiness and collapse into tears, or paroxysms of laughter, or fly into a rage, or dash for the nearest exit.

Goffman notes a special situation in which embarrassment may occur (1967:108):

> Often important everyday occasions of embarrassment arise when the self projected is somehow confronted with another self which, though valid in other contexts, cannot be here sustained in harmony with the first. Embarrassment, then, leads us to the matter of "role segregation." Each individual has more than one role, but he is saved from role dilemma by "audience segregation," for, ordinarily, those before whom he plays out one of his roles will not be the individuals before whom he plays out another, allowing him to be a different person in each role without discrediting either.

In the quotation above Goffman uses the term "role" to refer to a self presentation. Thus although we, along with Goffman, have separated the concept of "self" from that of "role," the self is in effect a personal role. The personal role played by an individual can vary from group to group, with perhaps the best-known example being that of Dr. Jekyll and Mr. Hyde. The state of embarrassment is also, in effect, a role that provides a transition from one self presentation to another. This way of considering emotions has been put forward by Sarbin (1984) and will be discussed in greater detail in Chapter 8 on actors and roles.

IMPRESSION FORMATION IN THE SHETLAND ISLANDS

Whenever an individual appears before others, the behavior of the individual will influence the others' definition of the situation. Goffman (1959:6–7) describes some of the ways in which this may take place and gives examples from his research on crofters (farmers) in the Shetland Islands. Sometimes the individual will consciously act in a thoroughly calculating manner in order to give the kind of impression to others that is likely to evoke from them the specific response that the individual desires. Sometimes the individual will be calculating in actions but be relatively unaware that this is the case. On other occasions the individual may be acting in a certain way because that is required by a social role.

When other members of a group know that an individual is likely to present the self in a favorable light, they may divide what they witness into two parts: a part that is relatively easy for the individual to manipulate at will, primarily verbal expressions, and a part that the individual is less likely to control, mainly nonverbal behavior. The others may use the impression given by the ungovernable aspects of the individual's behavior as a check upon the validity of what is conveyed by the governable aspects. In this case there is an asymmetry in the communication process, since the individual is attending to one channel of communication while the observers have access to two channels.

In the Shetland Islands, Goffman observed that one crofter's wife, while serving native dishes to a visitor from the mainland of Britain, would listen with a polite smile to his claims that he liked what he was eating. At the same time she would take note of the rapidity with which he lifted his fork to his mouth and the gusto expressed in chewing his food, using these signs as a check on the stated feelings of the eater.

Given the fact that others are likely to check up on the more controllable aspects of behavior by observing the less controllable aspects, the individual will sometimes try to exploit this possibility by guiding what are presumably the uncontrollable aspects of behavior. In the Shetland Islands, a neighbor dropping in to have a cup of tea would ordinarily wear at least a hint of an expectant warm smile when passing through the door of the cottage. Since one could observe the approach of a visitor without being seen, islanders sometimes took pleasure in watching the visitor drop whatever expression was manifest and replace it with a sociable one just before reaching the door. However, some visitors, aware that they would be observed, adopted a social face a long distance from the house, thus ensuring the projection of a constant image.

This kind of control of impressions on the part of the individual reinstates the symmetry of the communication process. It could set the stage for a kind of information game involving a potentially infinite cycle of concealment, discovery, false revelation, and rediscovery. However, Goffman reassures us that ordinarily definitions of the situation projected by the participants in an activity are sufficiently attuned to one another so that open contradiction will not occur. Each participant is expected to convey a view of the situation that others will be able to find at least temporarily acceptable. This "working consensus" varies with the setting. For example, if two friends are having lunch, a reciprocal show of affection, respect, and concern for the other is maintained. In contrast, a specialist often maintains an image of disinterested involvement in the problem of a client, while the client responds with a show of respect for the competence and integrity of the specialist.

APPEARING SANE IN A MENTAL HOSPITAL

Messinger (1962:101–2) observed behavior in a mental hospital where the patients would attempt to project a normal "self," only to worry later whether they were really normal or not. Like others "onstage," the patients regarded their own activities as potential "performances"—as potential means for creating and maintaining a "character" for the benefit of others. At times they would use their activities in this way. However, the patients faced a dilemma. The show that was staged concerned a fundamental matter, a matter that would not ordinarily be, or need to be, staged, namely, "normality." This was an aspect of self that the patients wanted others to take for granted once recovery had been achieved. More important, "normality" was an aspect of the self the patients themselves also wanted to take for granted again. Thus regarding normal behavior as a "performance" interfered with the patients' own assessment of being normal again.

Thus a patient might enact a "normal character" and succeed in taking in the audience, only to discover later that in the process the patient was even less convinced than ever about the "reality" of his or her own "normality." Anticipating this sort of conflict, a patient might pointedly avoid "performing." For example, one woman patient said that if she decided to, she could easily get out of the hospital, since she had learned what she was supposed to say and do to accomplish this. However, she said that to do these things was to deny one's "own self" and what "one felt." Moreover, what a patient had been saying and doing might be defined by an authoritative other as "performing," thereby provoking the conflict. Another patient said that when one of the doctors told her that she was "painting the picture too rosy," she realized that she had been trying to impress hospital staff just to get out of the hospital, and this frightened her.

Similar observations have been made of prisoners who work to demonstrate institutionally approved character and change to the prison staff—in the prisoner's words, "to show who you are" (Watson, 1982).

MONODRAMA

One type of presentation of self takes the form of a *monodrama* in which the protagonist takes several parts by implying that several voices are speaking. Harré (1979:220–23) gives some examples of this.

One type of monodrama occurs when a person feels some disparity between the way that he or she would like to be seen and the way that the person's actions may be understood. A solution is to speak in a way that implies a cast of characters rather than a single individual. For example, someone may say, "you never know, do you?" In this comment, three characters are implied: the speaker, the person being addressed (the second "you"), and the first "you" which represents abstract humanity. The proper response to the question is "no, you do not," rather than "no, I do not." The "you" who does not is the one of abstract humanity.

To cover up some failing a person may say "I talked myself into it." Thus the person's reluctance to act or weakness of character is masked in part by attributing it to a separated and rather feeble-willed person, the "me" who can be controlled by the "I," the primary actor in the little drama. Thus, as Harré (1979:222) observes, monodrama is "a way of talking that facilitates self-mastery by separating, as into another person, situation-relative undesirable personal characteristics."

ALTERCASTING

Even a person playing only one part in a drama may select or induce others to play parts that will reinforce the desired image of the self. The term *altercasting* has been used to describe the behavior of a person who induces others to play preferred auxiliary roles (Weinstein and Deutschberger, 1963).

Burns (1972:139) includes this phenomenon as part of her observation that ordinary social conduct at its most routine or informal, the kind of conduct that takes place in families or among friends, is composed and contrived. Each person acts as a theatrical producer by presenting a version of self and handing out parts to others as co-actors or as members of an audience. Because there is no formal artistic control, Burns notes that there is a certain amount of unpredictability, clumsiness, and recalcitrance among actors and audience. Climaxes do not always occur; scenes do not "come off"; appropriate lines are not spoken; and relationships often disintegrate, because, as in a theatrical improvisation, the actors dry up. Moreover, there is no way, short of dying, in which a person can end a personal performance. Friends can be discarded, or a move made to a different place, but the person can rarely bow out of all human interaction. Burns concludes that action in the theater is contrived for an occasion, for the duration of a play, whereas social action is perpetually contrived.

SUMMARY

Goffman, and others following his lead, have focused on the ways in which an individual presents an image of self to others and tries to discover the others' true selves. The basic approach of one individual to another is one of distrust since each individual is trying to save face. Throughout the self presentation each individual must also be a director, critic, and audience member as well as an actor in order to monitor and adjust the performance.

Goffman describes two kinds of face work, that is, actions taken by a person to make whatever is being done consistent with the preferred face: (1) avoidance processes—using go-betweens or other ways of avoiding actions and situations that would lead to a loss of face; and (2) corrective processes—giving presents, saying "excuse me", or in other ways making amends for the breach of face. A person who does something that is quite out of line with the expectations of others may feel flustered and show outward signs of embarrassment. This lack of composure may be acknowledged by others, or they may choose to ignore it. If the feeling of embarrassment is too great, the person may burst into tears, become angry, or show some other emotion. These emotional states are in effect a bridge that allows the individual to move over the break in the performance of self presentation.

Observers may use the ungovernable, mainly nonverbal, behavior of an individual as a check upon the validity of the governable aspects, primarily verbal expressions. The ordinary definitions of the situation projected by participants in an activity are usually sufficiently attuned to each other so that continuous checking is not necessary and open contradictions do not occur.

Messinger observed that some patients in a mental hospital attempted to project a normal self, only to worry later whether they were really normal or not.

Harré refers to a type of self presentation where the protagonist takes several parts by implying that several voices are speaking as a monodrama. This is a way of talking that facilitates self-mastery by separating, as into another person, undesirable personal characteristics. Even if a person plays only one part in a drama, the person may engage in altercasting by selecting or inducing others to play parts that will reinforce the desired image of the self.

4

Teams

Erving Goffman

[Since Goffman has provided the most extensive discussion in the dramaturgical literature on the part played by teams in suporting an individual's performance, in this chapter we bring in Goffman as a member of our team by quoting directly selections from his chapter "Teams" (1959:77–105). The reader should note that Goffman was writing in the late 1950s when the new gender consciousness had not yet arisen. Thus, following the custom of the time, he refers to the general person as a male. If he were writing this today, we are confident that he would modify his self presentation to be in accord with the new "working consensus."]

In thinking about a performance it is easy to assume that the content of the presentation is merely an expressive extension of the character of the performer and to see the function of the performance in these personal terms. This is a limited view and can obscure important differences in the function of the performance for the interaction as a whole.

First, it often happens that the performance serves mainly to express the characteristics of the task that is performed and not the characteristics of the performer. Thus one finds that service personnel, whether in profession, bureaucracy, business, or craft, enliven their manner with movements which express proficiency and integrity, but, whatever this manner conveys about them, often its major purpose is to establish a favorable definition of their service or product. Further, we often find that the personal front of the performer is employed not so much because it allows him to present himself as he would like to appear but because his appearance and manner can do something for a scene of wider scope. It is in this light that we can understand how the sifting and sorting of urban life brings girls with good grooming and correct accent into the job of receptionist, where they can present a front for an organization as well as for themselves.

But most important of all, we commonly find that the definition of the situation projected by a particular participant is an integral part of a projection that is fostered and sustained by the intimate co-operation of more than one participant. For example, in a medical hospital the two staff internists may require the intern, as part of his training, to run through a patient's chart, giving an opinion about each recorded item. He may not appreciate that his show of relative ignorance comes in part from the staff studying up on the chart the night before; he is quite unlikely to appreciate that this impression is doubly ensured by the local team's tacit agreement allotting the work-up of half the chart to one staff person, the other half to the second staff person. This teamwork ensures a good staff showing—providing, of course, that the right internist is able to take over the catechism at the right time. . . .

[RELATIONSHIP BETWEEN TEAM MEMBERS]

It is apparent that individuals who are members of the same team will find themselves, by virtue of this fact, in an important relationship to one another. Two basic components of this relationship may be cited.

First, it would seem that while a team-performance is in progress, any member of the team has the power to give the show away or to disrupt it by inappropriate conduct. Each teammate is forced to rely on the good conduct and behavior of his fellows, and they, in turn, are forced to rely on him. There is then, perforce, a bond of reciprocal dependence linking teammates to one another. When members of a team have different formal statuses and rank in a social establishment, as is often the case, then we can see that the mutual dependence created by membership in the team is likely to cut across structural or social cleavages in the establishment and thus provide a source of cohesion for the establishment. Where staff and line statuses tend to divide an organization, performance teams may tend to integrate the divisions.

Secondly, it is apparent that if members of a team must co-operate to maintain a given definition of the situation before their audience, they will hardly be in a position to maintain that particular impression before one another. Accomplices in the maintenance of a particular appearance of things, they are forced to define one another as persons "in the know," as persons before whom a particular front cannot be maintained. Teammates, then, in proportion to the frequency with which they act as a team and the number of matters that fall within impressional protectiveness, tend to be bound by rights of what might be called "familiarity." Among teammates, the privilege of familiarity—which may constitute a kind of intimacy without warmth—need not be something of an organic kind, slowly developing with the passage of time spent together, but rather a formal relationship that is automatically extended and received as soon as the individual takes a place on the team.

In suggesting that teammates tend to be related to one another by bonds of reciprocal dependence and reciprocal familiarity, we must not confuse the type of group so formed with other types, such as an informal group or clique. A teammate is someone whose dramaturgical co-operation one is dependent upon in fostering a given definition of the situation; if such a person comes to be beyond the pale of informal sanctions and insists on giving the show away or forcing it to take a particular turn, he is none the less part of the team. In fact, it is just because he is part of the team that he can cause this kind of trouble. Thus the isolate in the factory who becomes a rate-buster is none the less part of the team, even if his productive activity embarrasses the impression the other workers are attempting to foster as to what constitutes a hard day's work. As an object of friendship he may be studiously ignored, but as a threat to the team's definition of the situation, he cannot be overlooked. . . . Thus while teammates are often persons who agree informally to guide their efforts in a certain way as a means of self-protection and by doing so constitute an informal group, this informal agreement is not a criterion for defining the concept of the team. . . .

A final comment must be added on what a team is not. Individuals may be bound together formally or informally into an action group in order to further like or collective ends by any means available to them. In so far as they co-operate in maintaining a given impression, using this device as a means of achieving their ends, they constitute what has here been called a team. But it should be made quite clear that there are many means by which an action group can achieve ends other than by dramaturgical co-operation. Other means to ends, such as force or bargaining power, may be increased or decreased by strategic manipulation of impressions, but the exercise of force or bargaining power gives to a set of individuals a source of group formation unconnected with the fact that on certain occasions the group thus formed is likely to act, dramaturgically speaking, as a team.(Similarly, an individual who is in a position of power or leadership may increase or decrease his strength by the degree to which his appearance and manner are appropriate and convincing, but it is not claimed that the dramaturgical qualities of his action necessarily or even commonly constitute the fundamental basis of his position.)

[MAINTAINING A LINE]

If we are to employ the concept of team as a fundamental point of reference, it will be convenient to retrace earlier steps and redefine our framework of terms in order to adjust for the use of team, rather than individual performer, as the basic unit.

It has been suggested that the object of a performer is to sustain a particular definition of the situation, this representing, as it were, his claim as to what reality is. As a one-man team, with no teammates to inform of his decision, he can quickly decide which of the available stands on a matter to take and then wholeheartedly act as if his choice were the only one he could possibly have taken. And his choice of position may be nicely adjusted to his own particular situation and interests.

When we turn from a one-man team to a larger one, the character of the reality that is espoused by the team changes. Instead of a rich definition of the situation, reality may become reduced to a thin party line, for one may expect the line to be unequally congenial to the members of the team. We may expect ironic remarks by which a teammate jokingly rejects the line while seriously accepting it. On the other hand, there will be the new factor of loyalty to one's team and one's teammates to provide support for the team's line.

It seems to be generally felt that public disagreement among the members of the team not only incapacitates them for united action but also embarrasses the reality sponsored by the team. To protect this impression of reality, members of the team may be required to postpone taking public stands until the position of the team has been settled; and once the team's stand has been taken, all members may be obliged to follow it. . . .

However, unanimity is often not the sole requirement of the team's projection. There seems to be a general feeling that the most real and solid things in life are ones whose description individuals independently agree upon. We tend to feel that if two participants in an event decide to be as honest as they can in recounting it, then the stands they take will be acceptably similar even though they do not consult one another prior to their presentation. Intention to tell the truth presumably makes such prior consultation unnecessary. And we also tend to feel that if the two individuals wish to tell a lie or to slant the version of the event which they offer, then not only will it be necessary for them to consult with one another in order, as we say, "to get their story straight," but it will also be necessary to conceal the fact that an opportunity for such prior consultation was available to them. In other words, in staging a definition of the situation, it may be necessary for the several members of the team to be unanimous in the positions they take and secretive about the fact that these positions were not independently arrived at. . . .

To withhold from a teammate information about the stand his team is taking is in fact to withhold his character from him, for without knowing what stand he will be taking he may not be able to assert a self to the audience. Thus, if a surgeon is to operate on a patient referred to him by another doctor, common courtesy may oblige the surgeon to tell the referring doctor when the operation will be and, if the referring doctor does not appear at the operation, to telephone him the result of the operation. By thus being "filled in," the referring doctor can, more effectively than otherwise, present himself to the patient's kinfolk as someone who is participating in the medical action.

I would like to add a further general fact about maintaining the line during a performance. When a member of the team makes a mistake in the presence of the audience, the other team members often must suppress their immediate desire to punish and instruct the offender until, that is, the audience is no longer present. After all, immediate corrective sanctioning would often only disturb the interaction further and, as previously suggested, make the audience privy to a view that ought to be reserved for teammates. Thus, in authoritarian organizations, where a team of superordinates maintains a show of being right every time and of possessing a united front, there is often a strict rule that one superordinate must not show hostility or disrespect toward any other superordinate while in the presence of a member of the subordinate team. Army officers show consensus when before enlisted men, parents when before children, managers when before workers, nurses when before patients, and the like. Of course, when the subordinates are absent, open, violent criticism may and does occur. . . .

It is apparent that if performers are concerned with maintaining a line they will select as teammates those who can be trusted to perform properly. Thus children of the house are often excluded from performances given for guests of a domestic establishment because often children cannot be trusted to "behave" themselves, i.e., to refrain from acting in a way inconsistent with the impression that is being fostered. Similarly, those who are known to become intoxicated when drink is available and who become verbose or "difficult" when this occurs constitute a performance risk, as do those who are sober but foolishly indiscreet, and those who refuse to "enter into the spirit" of the occasion and help sustain the impression that guests tacitly unite in maintaining to the host.

[TWO TEAMS]

I have suggested that in many interaction settings some of the participants co-operate together as a team or are in a position where they are dependent upon this co-operation in order to maintain a particular definition of the situation. Now when we study concrete social establishments we often find that there will be a significant sense in which all the remaining participants, in their several performances of response to the team-show put on before them, will themselves constitute a team. Since each team will be playing through its routine for the other, one may speak of dramatic interaction, not dramatic action, and we can see this interaction not as a medley of as many voices as there are participants but rather as a kind of dialogue and interplay between two teams. I do not know of any general reason why interaction in natural settings usually takes the form of two-team interplay, or is resolvable into this form, instead of involving a larger number, but empirically this seems to be the case. Thus, in large social establishments, where several different status grades prevail, we find that for the duration of any particular interaction, participants of many different statuses are typically expected to align themselves temporarily into two team groupings. For example, a lieutenant at an Army post will find himself aligned with all the officers and opposed to all enlisted men in one situation; at other times he will find himself aligned with junior officers, presenting with them a show for the benefit of senior officers present. There are, of course, aspects of certain interactions for which a two-team model is apparently not suitable. Important elements, for example, of arbitration hearings seem to fit a three-team model, and aspects of some competitive and "social" situations suggest a multi-team model. It should also be made clear that whatever the number of teams, there will be a sense in which the interaction can be analyzed in terms of the co-operative effort of all participants to maintain a working consensus.

If we treat an interaction as a dialogue between two teams, it will sometimes be convenient to call one team the performers and to call the other team the audience or the observers, neglecting momentarily that the audience, too, will be presenting a team-performance. In some cases, as when two one-person teams interact in a public institution or in the home of a mutual friend, it may be an arbitrary choice as to which team to call the performer and which to call the audience. In many important social situations, however, the social setting in which the interaction occurs is assembled and managed by one of the teams only, and contributes in a more intimate way to the show this team puts on than to the show put on in response by the other team. A customer in a shop, a client in an office, a group of guests in the home of their hosts—these persons put on a performance and maintain a front, but the setting in which they do this is outside of their immediate control, being an integral part of the presentation made by those into whose presence they have come. In such cases, it will often be convenient to call the team which controls the setting the performing team, and to call the other team the audience. So, too, it will sometimes be convenient to label as performer the team which contributes the more activity to the interaction, or plays the more dramatically prominent part in it, or sets the pace and direction which both teams will follow in their interactive dialogue. . . .

[SUMMARY]

A team, then, may be defined as a set of individuals whose intimate co-operation is required if a given projected definition of the situation [line] is to be maintained. A team is a grouping, but it is a grouping not in relation to a social structure or social organization but rather in relation to an interaction or series of interactions in which the relevant definition of the situation is maintained.

We have seen, and will see further [Goffman, 1959:106–255, passim], that if a performance is to be effective it will be likely that the extent and character of the co-operation that makes this possible will be concealed and kept secret. A team, then, has something of the character of a secret society. The audience may appreciate, of course, that all the members of the team are held together by a bond no member of the audience shares [although the audience itself may become a team]. Thus, for example, when customers enter a service establishment, they clearly appreciate that all employees are different from customers by virtue of this official role. However, the individuals who are on the staff of an establishment are not members of a team by virtue of staff status, but only by virtue of the co-operation which they maintain in order to sustain a given definition of the situation. No effort may be made in many cases to conceal who is on the staff; but they form a secret society, a team, in so far as a secret is kept as to how they are co-operating together to maintain a particular definition of the situation. Teams may be created by individuals to aid the group they are member of, but in aiding themselves and their group in this dramaturgical way, they are acting as a team, not a group. Thus a team, as used herein, is the kind of secret society whose members may be known by non-members to constitute a society, even an exclusive one, but the society these individuals are known to constitute is not the one they constitute by virtue of acting as a team.

Since we all participate on teams we must all carry within ourselves something of the sweet guilt of conspirators. And since each team is engaged in maintaining the stability of some definitions of the situation, concealing or playing down certain facts in order to do this, we can expect the performer to live out his conspiratorial career in some furtiveness.

5

Audience

Our consideration of the function of an audience for social interaction begins with Goffman's comparison of the differences between the roles of theatergoer and an onlooker in a theater. With Sarbin we then note that the audience need not be physically present to have an impact on an actor's performance, although the four functions of an audience that Sarbin identifies will have their full effect only when the audience is present. Finally we provide examples of the way in which social activities can be classified according to their relationship to an audience and whether the activity is real or primarily symbolic.

THEATERGOER AND ONLOOKER

The theatergoer who attends a staged performance has several types of activity to carry out, some before, some during, and some after the show. The *theatergoer*, as Goffman (1974:129–31) records, is the one who makes the reservations and pays for the tickets, comes late or on time, takes the intermission break, and is responsive to the curtain call after the performance.

Each theatergoer is also an *onlooker* who collaborates in the unreality on stage by sympathetically and vicariously participating in the unreal world generated by the dramatic interplay of the scripted characters. Goffman illustrates the difference between the theatergoer and the onlooker with examples of two kinds of laughter. Laughter by members of the audience in sympathetic response to an effective bit of buffoonery by a staged character can be distinguished from laughter that may greet an actor who misses a line, trips, or breaks up in some unscripted way. In the first case the members of the audience laugh as onlookers, in the second as theatergoers. Although the actors on stage proceed as if they had not heard either kind of laughter, the effect on the performer is presumably quite different. Sympathetic laughter may cause a performer to pause to accommodate the response, whereas the laughter at a slip may cause the performer to move on with the play as quickly as possible.

OTHERS AND SELF AS AUDIENCE

In the course of an everyday performance, Burns (1972:136–37) notes, the *audience* is not necessarily constant. Other persons involved in the action or nonparticipating individuals can be maneuvered into the position of acting as an audience—for example, the guests at a dinner party serve as an audience for the person telling an anecdote, or crowds play the part of spectators at a street fight or a police chase. It is also common for people to go out of their way to avoid an audience for scenes in which they may not appear to advantage, as when parents try to avoid quarreling or scolding their children in front of friends or even of strangers.

Mead (1934) identified another type of audience dwelling inside the self. There are assumed to be two parts of the self, the "I" and the "Me." Mead described the *Me* as an inner audience, observing, encouraging, or restraining the actions of the *I*. This is also a way of describing conscience or inner criticism. If a person is disgusted by his or her own behavior, the "Me" can be said to be providing an audience capable of criticizing and restraining the "I." Burns suggests that this audience can, like any other audience, be deceived, so that at times one can be taken in by one's own act: by a display of moral fervor or of grief.

REFERENCE GROUPS

Role enactment is sometimes directed toward an audience that may only be present in the mind of the actor (Sarbin, in Allen and Scheibe, 1982:55; or Sarbin and Allen, 1968:532). In the social–psychological literature these special kinds of audiences have been called *reference groups*. A reference group may be a single other person, a group, or a category of people. It may even be a nonexistent group or category of people—for example, the future generation. Mead (1934) and others writing with a dramaturgical perspective have used the term "generalized other" for the cognitive representation of an audience that stands for the norms of a group or society and thus has special importance in directing and controlling a person's behavior.

FUNCTIONS OF AN AUDIENCE

Sarbin (Allen and Scheibe, 1982:55–56; or Sarbin and Allen, 1968:534) summarizes four aspects of the functions of an audience:

1. *Consensual reality*: by accepting a role enactment as appropriate, the audience provides validation for the enactment. By their presence during the role enactment and their acceptance of the role as it is interpreted by the performer, the observers publicly confirm the reality of the role and thus create social reality. For example, the role of doctor is validated as the medical student performs in front of an audience of members of the medical school staff (Haas and Shaffir, 1982).

2. *Cueing*: the cue is a discriminative response from the audience that guides the performer's role enactment. For example, quizzical expressions from the audience provide a cue that the role behavior is ambiguous. Cues from an audience can also control the pace or intensity of an enactment. An audience may also "cue in" an actor concerning the most desired or effective course of behavior.

3. *Social reinforcement*: an audience has many ways of demonstrating approval or disapproval of role behavior. At a staged performance, it can give praise by applause, and censure by hisses, boos, and jeers. In everyday life, however, more subtle techniques of expressing approval and disapproval are commonly employed.

4. *Continual observation*: by continually observing an enactment, the audience contributes to the maintenance of role behavior over time. A person desiring to change a role finds this difficult without a geographical change. The actor must escape from the previous audience that helped to maintain and sustain the role enactment. If a person is playing several different roles, the audience can discriminate among them and ensure that a degree of distinctiveness is maintained among the roles.

PERFORMANCE IN RELATION TO AN AUDIENCE

Some instances of social interaction are *real* in that they have some actual function to perform, while others are more *symbolic* in that they are intended to give meaning beyond that implicit in the actual behavior (see De Man, 1984:209). Furthermore, an audience may be either absent or present. Goffman (1974:125–27) provides some examples of different types of audiences. He suggests that performances can be distinguished according to their purity—that is, according to the exclusiveness of the claim that the watchers have on the activity that they watch. Dramatic plays, nightclub acts, ballet, and much orchestral music are of the pure type, because without an audience there will be no performance. Contests and matches when presented for viewing come next, for the whole activity depends upon the contestants' acting as if the final score of the game is what drives them rather than the gate receipts. A little less pure are personal ceremonies such as weddings and funerals. As the most impure of all, Goffman ranks work performances—for example, at construction sites, where viewers openly watch persons at work who show no concern for the dramatic elements in their labor. In making these distinctions among performances Goffman refers to the official face of the activity, not its underlying character and intent. For example, political trials or wrestling matches may in fact be staged for television. Or, as Gusfield (1981:78) reports in his analysis of publicity about the drinking driver, the "facts" are often exaggerated to produce a heightened emotional involvement on the part of the public by suggesting that the problem is even more serious than the actual facts record.

As a summary of some of the points made above, especially with regard to whether events are real or symbolic and an audience is absent or present, the discussion in the following paragraphs suggests ways in which these variables may be used to classify types of social events (Hare, 1985:54–55).

An audience is crucial for a theatrical performance. As observers and critics of the theater have pointed out, there is no play until it is performed (there is only a script), and there is no performance unless there is an audience. Thus the main difference between theater and ordinary life would seem to be that in theater, no matter how real or imagined are the relationships between the actors who mount the stage, their main intention is to transmit an "illusion" to an audience. For the most part, in everyday life, the persons involved really do have relations to each other and really do have a task to perform, whether an audience is present or not. To the extent that this difference between the theater and everyday life holds, the analysis of theatrical activity and the use of theatrical concepts as metaphors should be most useful when the actions of everyday people are primarily intended to transmit an image to some onlooker, and least useful when the primary intention is to cooperate in reaching some goal.

The distinction between a theatrical performance that requires an audience and everyday life is eroded, however, if we consider that in everyday life often there is an audience present and the actors are aware of it, even if the audience consists just of members of the group who do not happen to be active at the time. Although the presence of subgroups was not stressed in many of the early laboratory studies of group discussion, there were typically two or three persons who did most of the talking while the others sat back as members of the audience. Even in a group of two, when a new image is presented, one person is in the role of the protagonist and the other a listener or member of the audience. It is only after the initial image has been presented that a complementary role can be assumed and the second person move out of the audience position.

REAL OR SYMBOLIC EVENTS AND ABSENCE OR PRESENCE OF AUDIENCE

Because we can expect that group members will pay more attention to the *meaning* of an activity if it is both symbolic and intended for an audience, and more attention to the *actual behavior* when the focus is on the completion of some task and there is no audience present, it should be possible to learn more about the effect of an audience if we arrange activities for comparison, as suggested in Table 5.1.

The left-hand column gives points along a continuum representing the actors' relationship to the audience. At one end of the continuum, at the top of the column, are placed actions that take place without an external audience, although members of the group who are not actively involved at a given moment may serve an

Table 5.1
Activities Classified by Nature of Event and Relationship to Audience

Relationship to Audience	**Nature of Event (examples)**	
	Real	***Symbolic***
no audience	family, work groups	meetings of cult members, fraternity initiations
provision for small audiences from time to time	kibbutzim or other experimental communities, industries that provide tours	rituals such as rainmaking
provision is made for audience	trials, weddings, amateur sports	religious observances performed by priests, medicine men, etc.
audience composed of persons who did not expect an enactment	crime in public places, terrorism	street theater
audience required for a performance	professional sports	stage plays, musical or dance shows, or other entertainments

Source: A. Paul Hare, *Social Interaction as Drama: Applications from Conflict Resolution*, p. 55. Copyright © 1985 by Sage Publications, Inc. Reprinted by permission of Sage Publications, Inc.

audience function. Additional points along the continuum include actions where a provision is made for a small audience from time to time, where an audience is expected but is not necessary, and where the audience is composed of persons who are trapped into an audience role, because they were not prepared for an enactment. The other end of the continuum is represented by actions where an audience is required for a performance. A further distinction is made in Table 5.1 between actions that are *real* in the sense that the group has some task to be accomplished and those that are primarily *symbolic* in that the behavior of the actors is intended to give a meaning beyond that implicit in their actual behavior. Thus at one extreme we have the family or a work group that carries out its activities without any audience in mind, unless there are relevant reference groups. At the other extreme we have stageplays or other entertainments, where the role relationships of the actors are governed by the illusion they wish to present and have little, if anything, to do with their actual everyday relationships.

SUMMARY

Goffman distinguishes two aspects of the role of a member of the audience. One is that of the onlooker who collaborates with the actors by sympathetically and vicariously participating in the unreal (symbolic) world the actors have created. The second aspect is that of the theatergoer who has several types of real world activity to carry out, some before, some during, and some after the show. If the actors are performing well or poorly, the theatergoer may comment on the fact.

In addition to persons who play the part of a formal audience, nonparticipating individuals in a group serve as an audience for those who are the focus of attention at a particular time. That part of the self, identified by Mead as the "Me," also serves as an inner audience for the activity of the "I." When actions are directed toward an audience that is present only in the mind of the observer, it is called a reference group. The reference group may be a single person, a group, or a category of people.

Sarbin has noted four aspects of the functions of an audience: (1) giving consensual reality by validating the enactment and confirming the reality of the role; (2) providing cues to guide the performer's role enactment; (3) reinforcing the role by approval or disapproval; and (4) contributing to the maintenance of a role over time by continual observation.

Events can be classified according to whether they are primarily real or symbolic and an audience is absent or present. At one extreme is the family or work group with a real task and without provision for an audience. At the other extreme is a stageplay where the role relationships of the actors symbolize an illusion they present to an audience.

PART II
The Dramatic Production

6

The Actable Idea

A drama begins with an "actable idea." In this chapter we will describe four categories of actable ideas that form a continuum (image, theme, plot, and script), with examples of each type of idea. These actable ideas need not be developed for each new occasion but are usually available in the form of a "pre-text" that provides a set of roles that would be appropriate for the situation. The chapter concludes with a summary of Bales' observations about unification and polarization around images in individual perceptual fields and social interaction fields.

IDEAS

The concept *actable idea* is taken from the vocabulary used in training directors of psychodrama. In *psychodrama* the director helps an individual who has a problem (the protagonist) to enact one or more scenes that represent aspects of the problem. The problem is first explored through an interview with the protagonist, but all the while the director is listening for the actable idea that will make it possible for the protagonist to set the scene, choose auxiliary players, and begin to reveal the problem in action rather than through continued description. Thus psychodrama, in common with many theories in social psychology, makes the basic assumption that social interaction is organized around some idea (Hare, 1985:17). Some of these ideas have a narrow focus, such as the stereotype of another person or group or the attribution of causality to a particular person or event. Some of the ideas cover a broader area, such as the expectations for the roles to be played in a given situation.

Burns (1972:140) suggests that any actable idea has two aspects: purpose and mode. The purpose involves some attempt to control others, and the mode is a way of defining the situation (or specifying the convention) that others will accept.

The ideas that provide a focus for social interaction can be placed along a continuum from those that are relatively simple and vague to those that are complex and provide detailed descriptions of the roles to be played. Four points along this continuum—"image," "theme," "plot," and "script"—are defined as follows (Hare, 1985:18–19):

1. *Image*: an emotionally loaded set of words, physical object, or event—for example, "ghetto," "blood bath," "bacchanalia," or "May Day." Images are more likely to guide interaction in informal groups or therapy groups where there is relatively little role differentiation and the work of the group is not rigidly defined. In groups of this type, once an image is presented, members tend to take sides, some being for and some against the image. Within each subgroup, the persons for whom the image is especially relevant will become leaders. If the positive and negative split is marked, the group may become polarized. On the next round a new image may unify the group.

2. *Theme*: a suggestion of movement over time, as in a musical score (Sharron, 1981). The theme includes both a direction of movement, with emotional tone, and a minimal set of roles to be enacted. Interaction organized around a theme is most likely to be found in instances of collective behavior, such as in the behavior of panic-stricken, riotous, or ecstatic crowds.

3. *Plot*: a more detailed scenario with more definition of roles to be followed and the stages a group must go through to reach a goal. Social movements in which people come together to do something about their common concern initially have this character—for example, when a political movement is formed to fight injustice (Gamson, 1985:616). The instructions given to subjects by a social psychologist before a laboratory experiment all suggest a plot (Katovich, 1984:61).

4. *Script*: the most complete set of directions for social behavior. The roles of each of the actors is specified as the play

develops through a series of acts. The behavior of persons in organizations takes this form. Berne (1972) and Steiner (1975) suggest that the interaction patterns of many persons can become so fixed that they can be considered "life scripts."

However, in small groups, instances of collective behavior, social movements, and organizations, there may be more than one script, plot, theme, or image being enacted at the same time. For some analysts, the conflict between these different enactments is a more fundamental phenomenon than the stability of the system. Lyman and Scott (1970:5), using the metaphor of a "game" for their analysis of social interaction, conclude that:

> If life consists of encounters, episodes and engagements among persons pursuing goals of which they are consciously aware, or about which they can be made aware, then it appears that the fundamental structure of human action is conflict.

IMAGES

Morocco (1979:15–18) describes the way in which images may be shaped in a self-analytic group as members collaborate in collective storytelling. Although the stories are about events that are apparently unrelated to the group, they are essentially metaphors, conceptualizing the problems facing group members and offering structures for member interaction. In the first meeting of a self-analytic group of high-school students that Morocco was observing, the members complained a good deal that the group leaders were not telling them what they should be discussing. Members began to recall a film of Harry Harlow's maternal deprivation experiments which all of them had recently seen in school. As several students added details, a dramatic image developed.

Although the film showed groups of monkeys as well as individual ones, the story developed by the group members pictured a single baby monkey trying to get nourishment from an unresponsive wire-and-cloth parent. Students referred to the monkey with "human" nouns and pronouns such as "somebody," "parents," and "kids" and ascribed human emotions to him with phrases like "a quivering mass of nerves" and "a cool guy." Their story concerned the way in which the monkey's social and sexual development was impaired by the lack of parental responsiveness.

The selection of details, language, and character of relationships linked the story not only to the film, but also to the members' concerns about the difficulty of learning to communicate in a group where the leaders provided so little personal attention. Morocco notes four stages in the development of a group image: (1) members experience uncertain, formless feelings; (2) a private image that expresses the member's feelings is introduced by one member; (3) other members diffuse and elaborate the image: and (4) the members' shared view is represented in a story, joke, or game.

THEMES

Cochran (1986:5) uses a concept similar to theme to describe an idea that may guide the behavior of an individual actor. He uses the term "position" to refer to "a portrait of one's order of being, at a time or over time." Cochran describes the playing out of a feeling of anger as an example of this type of "incipient story":

> In anger one is upset by an offense; one judges the moral violation, fuels it with all manner of evidence (actual or imagined), denounces the character of the offender, and is moved toward revenge, punishment, a balancing of the scales. To be angry is to plunge into a particular type of dramatic experience or way of being. The actual drama that unfolds might fulfill the angry position one has taken, or it might involve numerous types of obstacles, complications, and detours, including a transcendence or abandonment of anger.

Sarbin's (1984:32) suggestion that all emotions can be seen as "transitory social roles" provides further examples of action guided by themes (see Chapter 8).

PLOTS

Rubin and Friedland's (1986:27) description of a typical terrorist action could be classified as a "plot" since the principal actors and their roles and the sequence of events have become fairly predictable. The terrorists typically begin with some action involving heightened drama, such as hijacking an airliner, and then issue threats and a set of demands. The government involved usually responds by testing the credibility of whatever threats have been made and stalling for time. At this point the terrorists may attempt to prove that they mean business, perhaps by killing a hostage and imposing time limits, if this has not already been done. The government continues to stall for time, if possible, even as it explores the feasibility of using force. The government also tries to take advantage of the "Stockholm syndrome," the tendency for captors and prisoners to identify with each other as time passes. This growing closeness makes it less likely that the terrorists will carry out their threats to destroy the hostages if their demands are not met. The event usually ends with the government using force or conceding to one or more of the demands of the terrorists. The concessions may be made in public or behind the scenes, giving the terrorists what they want without making the government lose more face than is absolutely necessary. Throughout the action the reaction of the mass audience is important to both sides and is determined in part by the media coverage (Weimann, 1983). Members of the audience in sympathy with the government will share the view that the terrorists are actually terrorists. For those in sympathy with the terrorists they are "freedom fighters," the official representatives of a beleaguered minority.

Another example of a plot is provided by Victor Turner (1974) who, as an anthropologist, observed the Ndembu people of Zambia. He concluded that one of the most interesting properties of village life was the propensity toward conflict. Conflict was rife in the groups of two dozen or so kinsfolk who made up a village community. It manifested itself in public episodes of tension eruption that Turner called "social dramas." Not every social drama reached a clear resolution, but enough did for Turner to identify the "processional form" of the drama.

There were four main phases in a social drama:

1. A *breach* of regular social relations would occur between persons or groups. There is always something altruistic about the symbolic breach. Although the breach may be made by an individual, the individual acts or believes the action to be on behalf of other parties, whether they are aware of it or not.

2. Following the breach, a phase of mounting *crisis* supervenes, during which, unless the breach can be sealed off quickly, there is a

tendency for the breach to widen and extend until it becomes coextensive with some dominant cleavage in the widest set of relevant social relations to which the conflicting or antagonistic parties belong.

3. The third phase is *redressive action* when "mechanisms," informal or formal, institutionalized or ad hoc, are swiftly brought into operation by leading or structurally representative members of the disturbed social system. These mechanisms vary in type and complexity with such factors as: the depth and shared social significance of the breach, the social inclusiveness of the crisis, the nature of the social group within which the breach took place, and the degree of autonomy with reference to wider or external systems of social relations. The mechanisms may range from personal advice and informal mediation or arbitration to formal judicial and legal machinery, and—to resolve certain kinds of crisis or to legitimate other modes of resolution—to the performance of public ritual.

4. The final phase consists either of the *reintegration* of the disturbed social group or of the social recognition and legitimization of irreparable schism between the contesting parties. After the fourth phase, it is quite likely that the social structure will have changed in noticeable ways.

Each of the phases had its own form of language and behavior. Underlying the "structure" of processionalism is an "antistructure" of "communitas" (a bonding uniting people over and above any formal social bonds: see V. Turner, 1980, 1982a, 1982b, 1985:177–246; and Nieburg, 1981). Cohen (1981:144–237) describes many examples of dramatic occasions among the Creole people of Sierra Leone, such as weddings, funerals, and religious celebrations, that provide social bonding.

SCRIPTS

Abelson (1981:715) provides an example of the psychological reality of scripts by considering the following simple story: "John was feeling very hungry as he entered the restaurant. He settled himself at a table and noticed that the waiter was nearby. Suddenly, however, he realized that he'd forgotten his reading glasses." Intuitively, the significance of the glasses lies in John's implied difficulty in reading the menu. No menu has been explicitly mentioned, however, raising the question of where such an expectation comes from. Abelson's answer is that it comes from the "restaurant" script, activated at the first mention of entering a restaurant. That script contains a standard sequence of events characterizing typical activities in a restaurant from the point of view of the customer. (See also Mandler, 1984:75–112).

Abelson distinguishes between "strong" scripts, such as going to the restaurant, which involve learned associations between prior and consequent events, and "weak" scripts. A weak script consists of a stereotyped set of events that lacks consistent sequencing properties. For example, a typical circus performance presents trapeze artists, a lion tamer, jugglers, and so on, but there is no necessary order to the various acts. Ableson refers to the "circus" script in the weak sense of script.

Nelson and Seidman (1984:68) record several types of symbolic play among young children. One of these types they identify as "scripted" discourse, the most common conversational form accompanying pretend play. This strategy required participants to find an event whose structure was known to both participants. Once an event for play was agreed upon, children were able to develop the event throughout the course of their interaction. The presence of objects in a sandbox such as a shovel and a pail might serve to bring forth a particular script as a play theme, such as baking a cake. Once suggested, the script serves as a continuous background framework within which both participants can play their roles.

A large everyday network of "explicitly structural rules" may have a strong impact on dramatic events and actions. In particular, there have been "major reassessments of social action emerging from class, gender, sexual preference, disability, age, and race. Goffman (1977) places gender rules at the forefront of scripting" (M. J. Deegan, personal communication, 12 February 1987).

Berger and Luckmann (1967:75), in their analysis of the social construction of reality, underline the importance of the script in their observation that:

> Only through ... representation in performed roles can the institution manifest itself in actual experience. The institution, with its assemblage of "programmed" actions, is like the unwritten libretto of a drama. The realization of the drama depends upon the reiterated performance of its

prescribed role by living actors. The actors embody the roles and actualize the drama by representing it on a given stage. Neither the drama nor institution exist empirically apart from this recurrent realization.

PRE-TEXT

When an actable idea is presented in a group, the group members do not need to develop roles on the spur of the moment. Rather, as Mead (1934) and other social-psychologists in the "symbolic interaction" tradition observe, they bring with them conceptions of sets of role relationships that would be appropriate to enact for each type of idea. In the theater the dramatist refers to the written script of a drama as the *pre-text*. The actual staged performance is designated as the *text*. The play's script is a guide for action but not a substitute for it, as the actors are required to interpret the script in action. Lyman and Scott (1975:103–4) suggest that the ideas the individuals in real-life dramas bring with them concerning the appropriate roles for each situation can be considered to be a *pre-text*.

Given this pre-text, an individual may rehearse a performance mentally for some time before the action takes place—for example, when a student receives a notice to visit the office of the school principal. When this occurs, the student may use all of the time it takes to go to the office to try out different scenarios representing possible reasons for being called to the office, what the principal will say, and how the student might respond. But the mental activity does not end there. Just as some playwrights attend the performances of their own plays and rewrite the scenario in accordance with their new interpretation of the drama as performed, so also social actors "attend" the performance of their own acts and "rewrite" the mental "scenario" that had been developed before going on to the next act. Goffman's analysis of the presentation of self, summarized in Chapter 3, is an example of this process.

IMAGES AND INDIVIDUAL AND SOCIAL FIELDS

A set of images (as defined above) in the mind of a group member is hypothesized by Bales (Bales and Cohen, 1979:31–35) to constitute a *field*. This may be called the *individual perceptual field*. The perceptual field includes the evaluative reactions, or attitudes, of the individual toward the images as well as perceptions of the images.

When an individual's field of images is *unified*, the images tend to be perceived as similar in important respects (above all, in terms of their positive or negative evaluation), and their differences may be minimized. When a field of images is *polarized*, the images tend to be divided into two (or more) subgroups in the individual's perception and evaluation. The subgroups of images may be opposed to each other, and the differences between the subgroups may be exaggerated. Under some conditions there may be a tendency to unify the images within each of the polarized subgroups. Thus the tendencies toward unification and polarization may be working within the same individual field in relation to different sets of images.

Bales places his observations about images and fields within a general theory that suggests that individuals react to each other in terms of the similarities and differences that they see between themselves, between themselves and third persons, and between themselves and objects to which they and third persons are co-oriented. Each individual tends to subjectively "move" the self-image and the images of others in response to his or her perception of the total pattern of the images in the field. In addition to the images of persons and things talked about in the present group, the total pattern for the individual also includes images from past experience and other images aroused by things talked about in the group and in the environment of the group.

For the whole group the *social interaction field* is hypothesized to be a dynamic entity that includes all the individual perceptual fields, plus the overt behavior by means of which people attempt to communicate to each other the contents of their individual perceptual–evaluative fields. As Lyman and Scott have also noted, the overt behavior and meaningful content of the communication interact with and change the individual perceptual fields. This in turn affects the overt behavior in a circular process. The social interaction field includes more than can be observed or communicated and thus must remain a hypothetical entity, although it can be described in sufficient detail to serve practical purposes.

What can be observed in a social interaction field in a small group is the focusing of attention of some of the members on one set of words or some physical object or event, which the observer conceptualizes as an *image*. For example, the members of a group may become excited about an idea such as "the proper attitude to take toward authority." A social interaction field often tends to develop toward a clearer pattern over a period of time. The focal image presented may change as group members communicate about it. There often seems to be a patterning of the whole constellation of communicated images, including the members' images of each other, that tends toward *unification* or *polarization*.

Some patterns of polarization–unification are fleeting, lasting only a few minutes, some last a whole meeting, and some recur again and again. A given instance of polarization or unification has a noticeable onset in some identifiable event, object, or set of words, which functions as a focal image. The pattern of polarization and unification among associated images then amplifies in intensity and propagates over more individuals in the group in a rapidly rising growth curve. Group members pay more attention to this constellation of images than to anything else. However, underneath, individuals are still dealing with a multiplicity of images, feelings, and concerns that may break through into communication, and the existing pattern may collapse.

Thus, the polarization–unification pattern of a *social interaction field*, as distinct from that of an individual perceptual field, is maintained only by the immediate communicative interaction between group members. To the extent that the interaction is intermittent, with long time lapses between actions and reactions, the particular polarization–unification pattern will collapse. The common focus of attention will be broken as the images cease to exert unifying and polarizing influences on each other. As other images begin to command the attention of individuals, another pattern may form, or the group may discontinue interaction.

The term *collapse* is used to indicate that the time required for a pattern to break up and disappear is often less than that of its appearance and growth. A pattern may change markedly within a few moments. Thus field patterns often appear suddenly, mount in clarity and intensity, hold a steady pattern for a period, and then collapse. Some collapses are only temporary. A given pattern may be reinstated again and again if there is a problem in the group or its environment that demands renewed attention.

SUMMARY

Four categories of "actable ideas" can be placed along a continuum from those that are relatively simple and vague to those that are complex and explicit about the roles to be played:

1. *Image*: an emotionally loaded set of words, physical object, or event (example: Morocco's description of the development of a group image in a self-analytic group).
2. *Theme*: a suggestion of movement over time, including direction and a minimal set of roles (example: Cochran's description of the playing out of anger).
3. *Plot*: a more detailed scenario with more definition of roles and stages (examples: Rubin and Friedland's description of a typical terrorist action, and Sarbin's description of a "social drama").
4. *Script*: the most complete set of directions for social behavior; in some situations there may be more than one idea being enacted at the same time (examples: Ableson's discussion of "strong" and "weak" scripts, and Nelson and Seidman's description of symbolic play of young children).

Individuals bring with them to each situation a pre-text, a set of roles that would be considered appropriate. Thus they do not need to create new roles each time, but can adapt the roles that are traditional for that situation. After each enactment, the pre-text may be rewritten in the light of experience.

Bales describes the individual perceptual field as the composite of the images of persons, objects, and ideas in the mind of a group member. For the whole group the social interaction field includes all of the individual perceptual fields, plus the overt behavior by means of which individuals attempt to communicate with each other the contents of their individual perceptual fields. In a small group, members tend to focus their attention on an image or images. If there is only one image, and the group members all have the same evaluation of the image, the group is unified. If there is one image that some members value positively and others negatively—or two or more images, especially if they are opposed to each other—then the group is polarized. Groups tend to swing back and forth between unification and polarization. Any pattern may collapse rather suddenly since the time required for a pattern to break up is often less than that of its appearance and growth.

7

Staging

The opening paragraphs of this chapter include some general comments on the effect of staging on performance, especially with regard to Burke's concept of the "scene/act ratio" and the stage as a "frame" for action. The influence of particular settings is illustrated with examples from Edelman's accounts of political behavior and Cavan's descriptions of everyday behavior, especially social behavior in places for public drinking.

STAGE-SET

We begin our analysis of the importance of the stage, scenery, props, costumes, lighting, and all other aspects of the setting with Burke's (1945:7) observation concerning the *scene/act ratio*:

> The stage-set contains the action *ambiguously* (as regards the norms of action) and in the course of the play's development, this ambiguity is converted into corresponding articularity. The proportion would be: scene is to act as implicit is to explicit. One could not deduce details of the actions from the details of the setting, but one could deduce the quality of the action from the quality of the setting.

Thus if you enter a room that has many chairs arranged to face a raised platform with a speaker's stand, a microphone, and a few chairs behind, you will expect to hear a lecture. If there are banners or maps on the wall behind the speaker's platform, you may also be able to guess the topic of the lecture. In general, any *setting* suggests a mode of appropriate activity and thus a range of possible roles that an individual may play on entering the setting.

In the theater the setting is often changed to denote a new scene or a new act. In everyday life we also refer to needing a "change of scene" to initiate some new activity. Denton (1970) reports that Canadian Indians take visitors either to the kitchen or to the living room, depending upon which setting is judged to be most appropriate for a discussion.

Another function of the setting is to provide a *frame* for the action (Goffman, 1974). Frames are constructed in order to make sense of complex happenings of nature and the doings of persons. They help to answer the question "What is going on here?" An example of constructing a frame for social behavior is marking the shift from serious goal-directed activity to play. The message "This is play" (i.e. fun and games) may be delivered, by word, gesture, facial expression, or contextual marker and serves to frame, and thereby demarcate, one scene from another. The communication "This is play" frames a particular context and creates the conditions for special kinds of role enactment (Sarbin, in Allen and Scheibe, 1982:21; or Sarbin, 1976:17). Another example of the framing function is given by Hopper (1983), who observed that jurors at a trial pay particular attention to the time and setting of a crime in their social construction of the moral meaning of a felony.

POLITICAL SETTINGS

Edelman (1964:95–98) observes that the setting is especially important for political behavior. Witnesses of political acts are likely to be sensitive to their setting and judge it to be appropriate or inappropriate. The common element in such political settings is their contrived character. They are built to emphasize a departure from daily routine and provide a special heroic quality for the proceedings they are to frame. These settings are usually massive, ornate, and formal. Thus the courtroom, police station, and legislative chamber all have their distinctive dramaturgical features. (See Cohen, 1979; Gusfield and Michalowicz, 1984; Lofland, 1975.) As in the theater, the creation of an artificial space makes it possible to intensify, condense, and organize a wide range of connotations, free of the many irrelevancies, distractions, and qualifications that fill everyday life. Great pains are often taken to call attention to the setting and to present it conspicuously, as if the scene were expected either to call forth a response of its own or to heighten the response to the act it frames. Greater attention is given to managing the setting when the enactment is intended to impress a large audience (Young and Massey, 1978), to legitimize a series of future acts, or to establish or reinforce a particular definition of self for a public official. For example, the setting may include the wife of an official to assure the public that her husband is "moral" and therefore worthy of public trust (Gillespie, 1980).

Edelman observes that political settings are intended for enactments in the presence of mass audiences rather than of small groups. He gives some examples from presidential press conferences in the United States that changed with shift from radio to television (Edelman, 1964:100–1). Superficially, as represented by White House press secretaries, this change led to closer rapport between the president and the people. The most "distant," Franklin D. Roosevelt, held closed meetings with reporters. They were usually forbidden to quote him directly, and much of the information he imparted was labeled as background and therefore unpublishable. Some years later, Eisenhower seemed to move closer to the people when he allowed reporters to record the press conferences for later editing and broadcasting. Subsequently, John F. Kennedy's press secretary claimed that the live telecasts of press conferences that the president arranged allowed for even greater intimacy.

However, Edelman records that perceptive observers and reporters during this thirty-year period complained that the change had actually been in the direction of greater remoteness, less information, and far more contriving of impressions. Roosevelt did not have to concern himself with mass impressions. He was able to convey information, set off "trial balloons," and be fully responsive to questions when he wished to be. The emphasis was on information and close contact with reporters. When the president wanted to address a mass audience, he had to rely on other devices, such as the "fireside chat" over the radio.

This closeness diminished with the advent of television. The small screen presented a live performance that was merely a semblance of close contact. Although the picture might be in one's living room, the president was remote and in a frame. He was offering a performance. Unlike Roosevelt, who had been able to exchange words with reporters without an audience, later presidents' words became unchallengeable and unchangeable. In the televised news conference, reporters asking questions became supporting actors. The news conference had changed from being a channel of information to being an instrument for influencing mass opinion.

Geertz (1980) provides many examples of dramatic political behavior in nineteenth-century Bali. He calls nineteenth-century Bali a "theater state." Geertz concludes that political symbology—including myth, insignia, etiquette, palaces, titles, and ceremonies—is but an instrument of the purposes concealed beneath it or towering over it. The purpose is to support the real business of political, social domination (1980:122).

EVERYDAY SETTINGS

Following the lead of Goffman and others, Cavan has been especially interested in developing an "ethnography of bar behavior," based on fieldwork done in bars in San Francisco. Before presenting a few of her observations on the varieties of arrangements for sitting and standing in bars, we will quote, almost directly, her observations on the effects of settings on behavior (Cavan, 1966:3–7).

The round of daily life takes place in many familiar settings: churches, factories, restaurants, homes, parks, courts, and doctors' offices. Associated with each of these conventional settings are patterns of behavior routinely expected within the setting. Such behavior may be evaluated according to whether it is fitting and proper for the time and place and is independent of the individuals who occupy the roles. These behavior patterns define for the person the activity that can take place as a matter of course and without question. The patterns may also delimit who is or is not eligible to enter a given setting, the ways in which routine tasks are to be distributed, the varieties of "reputations" that can be accorded to those entering, and the kinds of fates that can be allotted to those present. Thus, these taken-for-granted, common-sense features of social organization are matters of practical interest. Whatever a person's goals may be, conventional settings represent one of the environmental features available as a field of action.

For most adults, the range of possible settings is quite extensive, and each day's activities may be viewed in terms of the settings they frequent regularly, those they enter only occasionally, and those they avoid. Sometimes there is no choice. Law or custom may require one's presence in one setting or exclude one from another. This, in turn, may depend on one's physical or social characteristics. For example, turkish baths or private clubs may deny entrance to persons who are not physically or socially qualified.

Participation in other settings may require commitment to a regular schedule of attendance. A place of work may have this character, where one's day-to-day presence may seem outside the range of choice as long as one is working for that particular firm.

However, most available settings provide alternatives that the individual may choose to use or avoid. The patterns of the settings denote not only the main activity or function, but also what secondary or alternative uses are fitting and proper within the setting. Thus the person is provided with a variety of locales where almost any of the mundane or eventful problems of social existence can be handled effectively and acceptably. The conventional settings provide the actor with the necessary stage, scenery, and props, and, most of all, as a matter of course and without question, the legitimacy to sleep, be amused, earn money, make love, clear one's name, daydream, or socialize.

Within any setting there are courses of action for which a person may be held accountable. Some may be of little importance, but others may be personally costly or beyond a person's capabilities. A person's presence in a given setting may require the person to be industrious, to run, speak softly, donate money, show grief, or disrobe, regardless of personal feelings or abilities. Thus the stage may be set in such a way that a person will be embarrassed, discredited, or degraded either by performing or by failure to perform.

The behavior patterns associated with a given setting may not be common knowledge. Some of the information about these patterns may only be available to "insiders." Settings may also be exploited in a way that is neither routine nor proper, but nonetheless possible. A student who appears to be taking lecture notes while actually doing an assignment for another subject is an example of using a setting to conceal an inappropriate activity.

Settings vary not only in the kinds of improprieties that can be covertly engaged in by those present but also in the kinds of improprieties that may be tolerated, the kinds of sanctions that may be meted out for various offenses, and the extent to which the sanctioning of offenders is a laissez-faire endeavor or one that is both formal and formidable. The ways in which a setting may be exploited with impunity may comprise one of its most important features.

SPACES FOR PUBLIC DRINKING

Cavan provides a description of bars in San Francisco (1966:88–89) and examines the effect of the arrangement of the setting on a group of persons engaged in public drinking. The persons who are present in a public drinking place customarily include many who are oriented toward the setting as something other than a place of work. The setting is expected to be "unserious," and therefore there is no definite group goal that requires the cooperation of particular sets of people.

Cavan describes the seating arrangements available for the patrons both along the physical bar and at tables and booths away from the bar. The ratio of bar seats to nonbar seats varied. In some establishments there were few if any facilities away from the bar; in others there were more places to sit away from the bar than there were along its length. At the two extremes were establishments that only had seats at the bar and those with only a service bar and no seating at the bar.

In settings where more of the seating was at the bar, the dominant arrangement of patrons was side by side. When more seating was available away from the bar, most of the patrons were seated face-to-face. The contrapositional seating would usually demarcate groups by separating them spatially from each other and orienting their members in a partial or fully face-to-face arrangement. In the case of lateral seating at the bar, members of any seated group were abreast of each other, and the distance separating different groups was no greater than the distance separating the patrons within groups.

Boundaries in any group with lateral seating were much less clear and easier to cross than those of a group in a contrapositional arrangement. Where the dominant seating arrangement was lateral, there was a tendency for groups and their encounters to be much more fluid, with group merging into group. Persons who were originally not part of any group were still in close proximity to others. In general, the mutual openness of bar patrons was heightened when patrons were spatially distributed in a lateral seating arrangement. Consequently, contact was more likely between unacquainted patrons seated along the bar than among those seated away from the bar.

Both the vagueness of group boundaries and general proximity contributed to heightened expectation that contact between the unacquainted would take place. In addition, the fact that the average distance between patrons at the physical bar was typically less than that between patrons seated away from the bar made contact more likely along the bar than away from it.

SUMMARY

Burke uses the term "scene/act ratio" to refer to the fact that each setting implies a range of behavior that is appropriate for that setting. The scene need not be changed physically to introduce a different mode of enactment. The frame for the action can be introduced vocally—for example, with the statement "this is serious" or "this is play."

Edelman gives examples of political settings that are built to emphasize a departure from daily routine and provide a frame with a special heroic quality. Political settings are usually constructed for mass audiences rather than face-to-face groups.

Cavan provides observations of varieties of arrangements for sitting and standing at bars. She notes that for most adults the range of possible settings available for the daily round of activity is quite extensive and provides the necessary stage, scenery, and props for almost any type of activity. In public drinking places, contact between persons is more likely between persons seated at the bar than between those seated away from it.

8

Actors and Roles

Our chapter opens with a description of each of the basic dramatic roles that may be played during a performance. Next, with Sarbin, we note the various aspects of role enactment that might be included in a complete analysis. Ralph Turner then brings us back to a consideration of the self with the results of his research on the self–role merger. This is followed by a diagram illustrating the possible conflicts that may arise when one has to play several roles at the same time. We conclude with a description of the process of moving in and out of a role and the way in which emotions may serve to bridge breaks in role performance.

DRAMATURGICAL ROLES

Because all behavior in a given situation is essentially behavior in role, it is useful to have a set of generalized dramatic roles that one can look for when observing social interaction (Hare, 1985:20, 48–51). The role of the audience member has already been described in Chapter 5. For any enactment there must be at least one person acting as *protagonist*, the theme carrier, and one *auxiliary* player. The auxiliary player may take a role in opposition to the protagonist as an *antagonist*, or play a supporting role, or be a member of a *chorus*. The protagonist may also provide the script and the direction for the performance, but the roles of *playwright* and *director* can be played by different persons. In addition there may be *backstage staff* who set the stage and support the players by providing costumes, makeup, and props. In any event, one person may play several roles, and several persons may play the same role.

The *playwright's* role is to provide the image, theme, plot, or script that guides the interaction. The playwright need not be present at the time of the action. In many small group settings the protagonist is also the playwright. In some cases, as in a mass demonstration or riot, the playwright may be visible in the audience if one knows where to look. Or the playwright, in the form of a provocateur, may be well hidden. In cases of terrorism, the person who inspired and planned the action may take pains not to be anywhere near the scene at the time of its implementation. In any event, it is helpful for the analysis of a case, and for any form of intervention, to know whether or not the principal actors are carrying their own themes or are attempting to be the heroes, villains, or fools in someone else's drama.

The major part of the role of *director* in the theater is to prepare the play for the stage. The work begins on first reading the play. Miles-Brown (1980:22) has indicated some of the initial tasks of the director:

1. Find the theme.
2. Observe the plot, subplot, and subtext.
3. Locate the dramatic climaxes.
4. Understand the style, characters, and relationships.
5. Visualize the staging.

The director continues to function during the actual performance by "side coaching" the actors before they go on stage, when they are in the wings during a performance, or at the end of the performance after the audience has left. There are everyday interactions where the person playing the director's role may be easily identified, such as a military commander, work supervisor, athletic coach, or master of ceremonies. However, in other settings, such as large protest demonstrations, the key government officials who are directing the government's response, and the persons who are directing the protest, if there are any, may not be visible to the audience or to each other. Electronic communication equipment makes it possible for the director to be in contact with many persons without being noticed. In small casual groups, a full-time director may not be needed. The role may be assumed by one or more members of the group as it is needed. If the activity is complex, as in the theater, the role of director may be shared by a number of people who have different functions.

If the group is not autonomous but is responsible to an individual or an organization that provides funds and sets overall guidelines for action, then the group can be said to have a *producer*. In the theater the producer provides the backing for the play. The influence of the producer may not be apparent to the audience, but financial limitations may well have determined the size of the cast and the elaborateness of the setting.

The central roles for the actors may include one or more *protagonists* who present the major images that guide the interaction and one or more *antagonists* whose major function is to oppose them. In serious situations (tragedies and melodramas), these are the heroes and villains; in expressive situations (comedies and farces), these are the fools. The supporting players, or *auxiliaries*, may have individual roles in support of a protagonist or an antagonist, or some of them may act together as a *chorus*.

The *chorus* played an important part in early Greek dramas, held in large amphitheaters without amplification for the sound, where masses of people and voices were used to underscore important aspects of the drama. Choruses still exist formally in music and dance. In small groups several individuals may act as a chorus as they "oh" or "ah" simultaneously. In larger gatherings the chorus function is performed by those who chant, sing, or dance in unison. As Van Laan (1970:17–18) has noted for the theater, the chorus may concentrate the spectators' emotions on particular themes, and their attention on particular events. The chorus may provide an emotional sounding board by expressing in its physical and verbal responses the protagonist's hopes and fears.

With the exception of the playwright, the other roles cited above are limited in the extent to which the person playing the role can creatively influence the definition of the situation. The playwright can introduce the highest level of creativity by providing a new understanding, or a process, or an event. The director can, at most, provide a further interpretation of the definition of the situation given by the playwright. For the actor, some creativity is still required in playing the role, but it is unlikely to go beyond the skill level as the actor brings to bear techniques and personal experience in the interpretation of the role.

ROLES AND ROLE ENACTMENT

Since the concept of *role* is central for sociology and social psychology, a mass of literature has accumulated on this subject, although in most cases the role is not described in its dramaturgical context. Rather, the focus of role theory has been on *ascribed roles* (such as those based on gender or kinship) or *achieved roles* (such as those based on knowledge or skill) and the variations in these roles that accompany stages in the life cycle. For Sarbin, role enactment (or social interaction) is the bridge between the individual and the group, between personal history and social organization. In his discussion of role theory, he provides a number of concepts that are useful in identifying the general aspects of roles (Allen and Scheibe, 1982:37–57; or Sarbin and Allen, 1968). Sarbin begins his observations about social behavior by asking questions about the appropriateness, propriety, and "convincingness" of the enactment of a role:

1. Is the conduct appropriate to the social position granted to or attained by the actor (ascribed or achieved)? That is, do the performances indicate that the actor has taken into account the ecological context (setting) in which the behavior occurs? In short, has the actor selected the correct role?
2. Is the enactment proper? That is, does the overt behavior meet the normative standards that serve as valuational criteria for the observer? Is the performance to be evaluated as good or bad?
3. Is the enactment convincing? That is, does the enactment lead the observer to declare unequivocally that the incumbent is legitimately occupying the position?

Ralph Turner has made some similar observations and emphasizes that persons continually check to see if the roles are appropriate for the situation.

> Actors will behave as though they and others with whom they interact are in particular roles as long as the assumption works by providing a stable and effective framework for interaction. They test the assumption by continuously assessing one another's behavior, checking whether that behavior verifies or validates the occupancy of a position by corresponding to expectations and by demonstrating consistency. (Stryker, 1981:20)

These observations could be made about any type of role from the most formal roles in organizational settings to the more ephemeral roles that a person might take in some of Berne's games (1964). However, they would appear to be more easily applied at the formal end of the continuum.

Sarbin goes on to identify three dimensions of role enactment:

1. The number of roles (played by an individual in different groups or the distribution in a single group).
2. Organismic involvement (the amount of effort put into the role).
3. Preemptiveness (the relative amount of time a person spends in a role).

Other concepts that Sarbin finds useful in role analysis include the following:

1. *Role expectations*: the rights and duties of a social position that is involved with complementary positions in a role set.
2. *Role location*: a cognitive process by which a person determines "who is that?" and "who am I?" in terms of a role system.
3. *Role demands*: the range of possible role behaviors required of a person in a given setting.
4. *Role skills*: physical and psychological readiness to perform some task at some given level of competence. Skills are both cognitive (taking the role of the other) and motoric (posture, movements, facial expression, and tone of voice).
5. *Self–role congruence*: the self is the "experience of identity arising from a person's interbehaving with things, body parts, and other persons" (Sarbin, in Allen and Scheibe, 1982:52). Role enactment is more effective when the requirements of the role are congruent with self-characteristics.

SELF–ROLE MERGER

Ralph Turner is also concerned with the relationship between the self and the role. He suggests that an understanding of the extent of the merger between the self and the role in any situation is important for an understanding of symbolic interaction (Stryker, 1981:20–22). Along with Sarbin, Goffman, and others, Turner observes that our self conceptions arise out of interaction with others, and we present ourselves to others in the light of these conceptions.

The roles we play have two main goals: to achieve group goals efficiently, and to achieve personal reward in the form of validation of self-esteem and reinforcement from others. Turner's research on the self–role merger reveals that people's ideas about their "real selves"—that is, about who and what they really are—depend upon whether their ideas about themselves have an "institutional" emphasis or an "impulse" emphasis. If they have an institutional emphasis, people will see their real selves in feelings, attitudes, and actions that are anchored in institutions. They will recognize their real selves in action when accepting group obligations. In contrast, people who have an impulse emphasis will see their real selves in untamed impulse with conformity to institutional norms occurring at the expense of their true selves. Turner finds that over the past several decades there has been a major shift in American society from institution to impulse.

MULTIPLE ROLES

As Sarbin has indicated, the same person may play many roles. Sometimes these roles are played at different times and in different places, sometimes they are played in the same place in succession, and sometimes they must be played simultaneously much as a juggler keeps several balls in the air at the same time.

A representation of the activity of a single individual is given in Figure 8.1. In this fictitious example the person is a married woman who with her husband and two sons is spending the weekend with her mother. When all the family is engaged in the same activity, she has at least three roles to play simultaneously: she is a mother, a wife, and a daughter. The task could also involve her professional skills as a social worker, or her relationships with friends, or any other role relationships concerned with persons who may be present or not present at the time. For each role there is a reciprocal role or set of roles (i.e. mother–father–children, wife–husband, daughter–mother) and a reference group composed of persons playing the same role. Also included in the diagram is the person's own personal role of "self," that serves as a basis for any role performance.

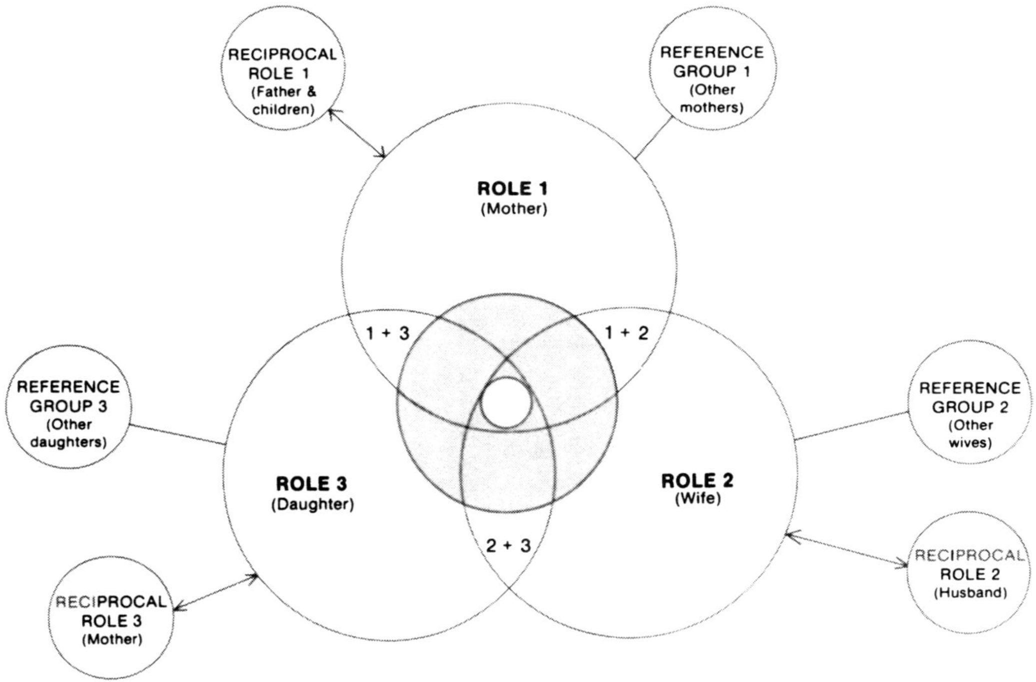

Figure 8.1
Multiple roles. (The shaded area represents the self.)

Since each of these roles requires a different set of behaviors, and the expectations of the person playing a reciprocal role may be different from the expectations of the reference group of persons playing the same role, there is a high probability of role conflict. One way to avoid role conflict would be for the person to perform only those behaviors that lie in the intersection of all of the sets of expectations for the various roles and the self. However, the more usual practice is to attempt to play only one role at a time and preferably in another part of the action space or on another stage altogether.

Goffman (1981:155–56) provides an example of a person dealing with several roles at the same time by a rapid alternation of talk to each of the counter-players in turn. Throughout an auction, an auctioneer may intersperse the utterances he directs to the audience with several streams of out-of-frame communication: reports on each sale spoken through a microphone to a recording clerk in another room, instructions to assistants on the floor, greetings to friends, and responses to individual buyers who approach with quiet requests for updating.

FROM WARM-UP TO ROLE CONSERVE

Sarbin, Turner, and others who have written about roles take a cross-sectional view. That is, they tell us something about the content of a role or the problems involved in its enactment, but not how a person moves in and out of a role. Based on Moreno's (1953) work in psychodrama, Yablonsky (1953:351–54) has outlined a longitudinal perspective on the development of a role that follows the person through the cycles of *warm-up* and *spontaneity/creativity*, ending with a *role conserve*. To our discussion of sequence we will add the period of *deroling* as a person comes out of a role before leaving behind a *role conserve*. We also note that before the person enters a role there is some initial role conserve that defines the rights and duties of the role as established by previous players.

Warm-up

The first period of enacting a role in a group involves some intellectual and often physical warm-up to the level of skill that the role requires and to the definition of the situation that the other group members share. Persons who take on roles to face emergencies, such as a firefighter or a member of a police force, may have only a moment to respond to a situation. Their crisis role may need to be so well rehearsed that they can do what is necessary almost without thinking. At the other extreme, the Olympic athlete may be given considerable time to perform warming-up exercises or even practice trials before the actual event. If rehearsal is required before playing a role, the rehearsal constitutes a separate phase. Here we are referring to warm-up during the enactment phase of the drama.

Sarbin's dimension of "organismic involvement" is also an aspect of the warm-up period. Some warm-ups may be superficial and require little organismic involvement if the situation has little meaning for the person involved. The involvement of an assembly-line worker may be low in contrast to that of a patient in a therapeutic session.

A person may have a mixed warm-up, as in the situation depicted in Figure 8.1, if the person has to warm up to several roles at the same time. Similarly one could describe as a mixed warm-up the case where a warm-up that may or may not be appropriate to the present situation is carried over from a previous situation.

Spontaneity/creativity

After the warm-up the person moves to the enactment period, which is characterized by some degree of spontaneity and creativity. Moreno's definition of spontaneity was "an adequate response to a new situation, or a new response to an old situation." If the response to the new situation is more than adequate or the new response to the old situation does something to redefine the situation for the persons involved, then some level of creativity has been achieved (Hare, 1985:23). Few roles are so explicitly defined that a person can mechanically act out the specifications within a situation. Even when the roles are very explicit, a shift in the situation may require some measure of spontaneity.

Yablonsky suggests that spontaneity is a basic concept for understanding behavior in action. For example, a worker on an assembly line might utilize in the activation of the role the minimum spontaneity, just enough to escape the boredom of mechanized activity. On the other hand, the research scientist would have to muster considerable spontaneity and creativity to play out the role. Within the same role two individuals may differ appreciably in their amount of spontaneity, as might be the case with two professors lecturing on the same topic. One might give a spontaneous presentation, adequately fulfilling the requirements of the classroom situation, while the other reads from a dog-eared set of notes.

Deroling

When it is time to move out of one role and on to another, a person goes through a process of deroling. As with warm-up, the deroling can be almost instantaneous, or it may take place over a period of time. An example of the rapid shift of dramatic roles would be seen at an after-dinner discussion of a social gathering. Persons shift from being the protagonist telling an anecdote, to acting as a supporting member, or as an audience member, without changing places or costumes, with only perhaps some shift in body position and level of attention. In contrast, in achieved roles, the deepsea diver cannot surface too fast without suffering the bends, and the professional actor may take some time to peel off the makeup, change costumes, and come down from the "high" of involvement in the performance. The processes of self reconstitution described in the next chapter provide more detailed accounts of the process of moving from one role to another. Every culture has developed elaborate ceremonies for the role changes that involve the major transitions for a person moving through the life cycle: birth, puberty, marriage, old age, death. There may be moments or longer periods when a person is between roles. Victor Turner (1974:50; 1982b:113) identifies these times as instances of "liminality"—transitions when a person is free to act out of role.

Role conserve

The product of the process of warm-up, enactment, and deroling is the role conserve. This is the new understanding of the role that has emerged or been consolidated in the previous enactment. As Ralph Turner has noted, not only the idea of the role but also a person's idea of self may also have changed as a result of a role enactment (Stryker, 1981:20–22).

ROLE FATIGUE

Barbour and Moreno (1980:187) quote Laurence Olivier as having advised aspiring actors: "Never perform longer than six months in one role, it's death." They observe that in many everyday situations people may be called upon to relate to others in roles that are no longer satisfactory. They identify this condition as one of *role fatigue* and define it as a loss of energy available for a role because of continued unproductive role performance. It is accompanied by a sense of physical, emotional, and intellectual exhaustion. Popularly referred to as "burnout," the phenomenon has been observed especially in the helping professions, which seem to require a person to give until they have no more to give. Physiological symptoms include extreme fatigue, tension, sleeplessness, low-back pain, headaches, and numerous minor ailments. Emotional symptoms include cynicism, irritability, nervousness, loss of enthusiasm, helplessness, frustration, rigidity, and suspiciousness. Behaviorally it is marked by lowered performance, lost initiative, overindulgence, boredom, absenteeism, and alienation.

Given this long list of symptoms that may be associated with "burnout," any director who is planning an enactment of some idea would do well to ensure that the participants are not kept in stressful roles for too long a period. Most high-stress organizations, such as military units, have recognized this need and provide for periods of "rest and relaxation." However, persons who are especially keen to initiate a new form of social interaction may find it difficult to let go of the idea, even for a brief period.

EMOTIONS: TRANSITORY SOCIAL ROLES

In Chapter 3 we noted that a person who suffers a loss of face because there is a break in self presentation may experience embarrassment or exhibit some other emotion. This emotional period serves as a bridge over the lapse in self presentation. Sarbin has identified a similar phenomenon when there is a lapse in the presentation of an ascribed or achieved role. He defines *emotions* as "transitory social roles that the actor assigns to a class of events called passions" (Sarbin, 1984:32). An emotion includes intentions for the future—that is, intentions to act in the interest of gaining status or power. For example, persons may intend to revenge themselves in anger, redeem themselves in shame, restore their dignity in embarrassment, or help another person in pity.

In any case, the period of emotion provides a transition from one role to another. In order to study "helping behavior," social psychologists have often set up situations in which someone appears to be in distress, to see how passersby will react. The passersby are in the process of enacting a different role connected with some goal other than helping someone in distress. Following Sarbin's insight, we would now look for a period during which the passersby are overcome by the emotion of pity before abandoning the former role and taking up the new role of helper. Or, to take an everyday example, a parent fixes some special food for a child. The child refuses to eat it, and the parent becomes angry and says and does things to let the child know this—at a minimum, saying "that makes me angry." Why the anger? Because the performance of the parent's role has been challenged by the child. The emotional period of anger serves as a transition to allow the parent to become reinstated in the parental role.

SUMMARY

Basic dramatic roles that are found in any enactment include those of the playwright who provides the idea that guides the interaction, the director who ensures that the action is carried out in accordance with the idea, and the producer who provides the backing for the performance. These roles may be separate, or they may be played by the protagonist who is the carrier of the idea. There may be an antagonist opposing the protagonist and several auxiliary players who support the protagonist or the antagonist. Some of the auxiliaries may act together as a chorus.

Sarbin suggests that one should begin the analysis of a role by asking about the appropriateness, propriety, and convincingness of the enactment. In addition, one can note the number of roles played by each individual, the amount of effort put into the role, and the relative amount of time spent in the role. Additional concepts that can be used to differentiate roles are: expectations, location, demands, skills, and self–role congruence.

Ralph Turner's research on the self–role merger reveals that people's ideas about who they "really are" depend upon whether their ideas about themselves have an institutional emphasis or an impulse emphasis. In the United States there has been a major shift during the past several decades from institution to impulse.

An example of the number of roles that one person may need to play at the same time is that of a wife and mother who is visiting her own mother with her family. Each of her three role relationships (wife, mother, and daughter) have counter players and reference groups that must be attended to. She must also have a concern for the relationship between all these roles and the self.

As a person moves in and out of a role, the periods of warmup, spontaneity/creativity, deroling, and role conserve can be identified. Roles differ in the amount of time and energy required to warm-up and to derole, and in the amount of creativity required for the enactment. The role conserve is a set of expectations for a role following an enactment. A new meaning may have been given to the role, and a new conception of the self may have emerged for the person acting the role. A person who remains in a role for too long a time under stressful conditions may experience role fatigue, a loss of energy available for role performance.

Emotions, as transitory social roles, can provide a period of intentional activity when there is a break in role performance or when a marked change in the situation requires a sudden shift of roles.

9

New Meanings

In this chapter we give examples of the ways in which new meanings can arise after the enactment phase of a performance. In each of these examples there is an intention to create a new meaning. The first example is Sarbin's description of the "self reconstitution" process by which a group provides a new meaning for an individual. The second example, Cole's description of the activities of the shaman and hungan, is a process through which an individual searches for meaning for a group. In the third example Gusfield describes "public dramas" in which public media or persons in authority create new meanings for a society.

NEW DEFINITIONS OF THE SITUATION

Just as every action begins with a definition of the situation, an idea that governs the action (Stebbins, 1986), so every action ends with a new definition of the situation (Perinbanayagam, 1974). Things are not as they were. After a theatrical production and for many everyday actions where an audience is present, the actors will have consciously tried to convey some new understanding of the situation to the audience. At the other end of the continuum—at group therapy sessions, cult initiations, religious conversions, and the like—audience members and actors may collude to give one of the actors a new understanding of the situation. Most events end with new meanings for both audience and actors. The new meaning may apply only to the given moment, such as the moment a person decides to purchase something in a store, or it may apply over a long period of time, such as a change of attitude about some ethnic group.

SELF RECONSTITUTION

The process by which an individual is brought to a new understanding of the self is described by Sarbin as *self reconstitution*. As an example of the process, Sarbin describes the Spiritual Exercises of Saint Ignatius of Loyola (Allen and Scheibe, 1982:120–21; or Sarbin and Nucci, 1973:188). This system of reconstitution of the self employs a death and rebirth theme. The exercises are carried out during a "retreat" in which four phases are identified as "weeks." These four stages of the reconstitution of the self are reminiscent of exercises in other Eastern and Western religions involving processes of catharsis, insight, and reorientation.

The exercises of the first week require the subject to meditate on sin and its consequences, to contemplate hell, and to meditate upon the subject's own death, picturing in detail the last moments of agony. The meditations of the second week involve the Savior as a means of salvation. The aspirant contemplates the humility, agony, poverty, and love of the Savior. During the third week the exercises seek to confirm the election to Christ—that is, working through to confirm the way of holiness. The fourth week is characterized by setting aside the dreadful thoughts and sadness, meditating instead on the life eternal.

These exercises in fact entail four phases that occur in the development of any new idea or in the development of any new group (Hare, 1982:76). They are the same four phases that have been identified in the development of a dramatic production. First one must have an idea, then find the means for enactment including a stage, then work out the necessary role relationships with the other actors, and then perform the activity. A fifth stage is to note the new meaning that follows the enactment.

In the case of the exercises of Saint Ignatius, the first phase develops the idea that the present self is sinful and in need of change. The second phase emphasizes the Saviour as the means that will facilitate change. During the third phase the aspirant experiences a new role relationship as one who is elected to Christ. The fourth phase consists of a trial period of enactment of the new relationship as part of the new "eternal life." The aspirant then leaves the retreat with a new meaning of the self, only to begin the process over again on a wider scale in attempting to integrate this new understanding of self into everyday activities.

Some methods of attitude change take a fairly soft line concerning the degree to which the initial self-image is sinful. For example, in the initial phase of the "Cursillio" (or Little Course) developed by Bishop Hervas in Spain to bring 40-year-old men back to active participation in the Catholic Church, the aspirant is reminded that he was once faithful but has fallen away. In contrast, in the methods of "thought reform" developed by the Chinese, considerable pressure was exerted to convince the captive that the captive did not have and never had "correct thinking" with regard to the nature of the ideal self and society (Lifton, 1961). Snow and Machalek (1984:1975) report that in some "new" religious movements the convert learns not only new practices for everyday life, but also how to describe "correctly" the process of religious conversion.

Harrison (1977), as he interprets religion in a dramaturgical context, observes that religious, social, and moral activities do not routinely achieve deeper levels of drama. However, when a "dramatic" event does occur, the primary participants and members of the active audience can recognize the moment as extraordinary, perhaps as an event of awesome historical significance. In these moments new religions and moral paradigms may arise and at such times routine role-playing and theatricality are eclipsed, although they never totally disappear.

In his review of many systems of self reconstitution, Sarbin identified five aspects that lead to the reconstruction of the self as preliminary to, or concurrent with, profound changes in conduct (Allen and Scheibe, 1982:123–29; or Sarbin and Nucci, 1973:185–88):

1. *Symbolic death and rebirth.* This theme has already been discussed in the early paragraphs of this chapter. For all these processes there is the expectation that certain personal behaviors will diminish or cease altogether, at the same time being replaced by a new set of overt behaviors and corresponding self-definitions.

2. *The group and the other.* The relationship between the convert and the group varies according to the degree of involvement and specificity of role perception. At one pole this relationship may take the form of an individual who comes in contact with a religious or millenial group. The group, in this case, provides a setting for change and, in addition to role models, also provides the conditions that demand certain performances from the initiate. Usually some individual or group is involved as the "Other," who is both a role model and a source of information.

3. *Ritual behavior.* There are two types of ritual behavior. One is ritual behavior per se, such as repeating prayers or regulating physical habits, which may serve to neutralize arousal and reduce strain during the process of conversion or may be required in the performance of new roles. The other type of ritual is to manipulate time to concentrate individual attention and to limit the span of attention—for example, by introducing a waiting period.

4. *Proprioceptive stimuli.* Emphasized in all systems are those positions and states of the body that allow the subject to shift perceptions of the world, as, for example, by kneeling, standing, lying, and prostrating. Fatigue states, cramps, hunger, and sleeplessness may be induced, and the subject's sensory dependence on external stimuli may be challenged. The alternation of periods of excitement and relaxation may also be used.

5. *Triggers.* Events of unusual texture or quality are likely to produce or enhance the process of conversion. The trigger is most effective if it occurs at the moment of transition in the death–rebirth process.

VISITING THE PLACE OF NEW MEANINGS

In self reconstitution the group helps the individual undergo an experience that will provide a new meaning for that individual. However, there are also occasions when an individual undergoes an experience that will provide a new meaning for a group. Cole (1975), writing about the theatrical event, draws on anthropological reports to document the fact that, at many points in history and in many parts of the world, people have believed that there is an "illud tempus," a time of origins, a period of creation. Creation continues because this is the place "where it is always happening." This illud tempus is a place in space, but it is also a place within the individual that is accessible through dreams and illusions. If members of a society want an interpretation of some current event, they can ask one of their members to journey to the illud tempus and bring back the new meaning.

In some societies there is a person, the *shaman*, who specializes in going into a trance state in which the person's soul is believed to leave the body and ascend to the sky or descend to the underworld to visit the illud tempus. Because the illud tempus is also within the person, the visit is also an inner journey. Because the shaman's double voyage is on behalf of an audience, the shaman makes it possible that "we go there."

A variation in this voyage is enacted by the *hungan*, a person who specializes in becoming "possessed." Although "hungan" is the Haitian term for a priest of a possession cult, Cole uses it to refer to all persons playing a similar role. The hungan is a human being whose presence becomes, through possession, a god's presence. The hungan makes it possible that "they come here."

Cole suggests that the two roles, of shaman and hungan, are in effect assumed by the same person at different times in the voyage. A person in search of insight is like a shaman going to visit a distant place. On reaching the place where creativity is always occurring, the person has a creative shift in perception, and then turns back, or "rounds." The return trip is in the role of hungan, one who is in possession of the new insight.

Cole (1975:54) describes *rounding* as "the moment when the quest can go no further, the spirit held no longer, the magic accomplish no more. To round at that moment . . . to become a hungan, a mere vehicle, is the price the shaman must pay for having attained his goal."

One does not have to be a shaman or a hungan to suggest new meanings to a group. When any new "actable idea" is presented in a group, whether brought forward from past experience or from an insight of the moment, an individual must make it "present" for the other group members. Unfortunately, if a group has not delegated one of its members to act on its behalf in the search for new meaning, the group may be reluctant to accept the insight once it is presented, especially if the individual has low status in the group.

PUBLIC DRAMAS

In the first two examples of the ways in which new meanings are revealed, the group provides a new meaning for an individual and the individual provides a new meaning for a group. A third way is for a group or set of individuals to provide a new meaning for another group or a wider set of individuals. Gusfield (1981) uses the term *public dramas* to identify situations where the apparatus of the public media, official authorities, or professional practitioners act to build up a sense of an orderly world. In Chapter 7, on staging, Edelman and others have provided examples of political events that are designed for this purpose, and the "social dramas" described by Victor Turner are more elaborate enactment of this type. Gusfield's primary example concerns the problem of persons who drink alcohol and then drive cars, but he also gives a number of other examples including U.S. President Nixon's performance after the revelations about the Watergate coverup that led to his resignation. (See also Gusfield, 1980:166–88).

Gusfield (1981:173) contends that, with regard to the issue of drinking–driving in the United States, both science and the law of drinking and driving create an orderly account of danger in the contemporary world. It is an account of the conflict between self-control and self-indulgence. There is a cognitive order in which drinking renders the individual motorist unable to control the machinery of driving adequately enough to avoid danger to self and to others. There is a moral order in which the use of alcohol is singled out as especially heinous, an act that the motorist could have and should have avoided. The drama of the "killer-drunk," as it is presented in the media and by other authoritative persons, involves the evil of persons who ignore the boundaries of prudent living and planning and by this action kill innocent victims and even themselves. The drama can be classified as a tragedy, since it involves the moral failing of a flawed person.

Gusfield's second example involves not an anonymous "killer-drunk" but the actions of a particular individual, in this case one who was president of the United States. Here, too, the public drama is seen as a mechanism for the creation of public order. Gusfield (1981:184–85) uses as his source of data the interview series that Nixon gave on television in the Spring of 1977, almost three years after his resignation.

The public attention given to the U.S. Senate investigation of the Watergate events and the House committee on impeachment, the actions of the jury, the indictments and the Judge's actions culminating in the evidence of the sound recordings, and the resignation, all created a dominant belief in the guilt of the president. Gusfield is aware that as a public drama Watergate had many meanings, but one of those was to dramatize the rule of law. This is the doctrine that no persons, even the president, ought to be beyond the responsibility for illegal acts. At stake, then, was the legitimacy of the political order, and the focus of inquiry could not have been more visible and dramatic since it was on the office of the chief executive, the highest elected post in the country. The focus was not on the legitimacy of this or that particular president, but of the presidency as an institution.

Near the end of a television interview Nixon dropped his posture of wronged innocence for one of humility and even shame. He admitted that he had let the American people down and that he would have to carry the burden for the rest of his life. Gusfield suggests that by covering himself with shame, Nixon helped to restore the sense of a consistent public order.

SUMMARY

Most dramatic events end with new meanings for both actors and audience. When the focus of the action is on a new understanding of the self by an actor, Sarbin refers to it as "self reconstitution." An example is a religious retreat where the participant goes through four phases: identifying the self as sinful, accepting the Savior as the means of change, experiencing a new role relationship, and enacting the new relationship for a trial period. Thus the participant has gone through the same four phases that have been identified in the development of any dramatic production or other type of group: develop an idea, find the means for enactment including a stage, work out the role relationships, and perform the activity. The fifth phase is the realization of a new meaning that may begin the process over again.

In his review of many instances of self reconstitution, Sarbin has identified five aspects that are important: (1) there is a symbolic death and rebirth, (2) another person or group provides a role model and a source of information for the reconstruction, (3) ritual behavior serves to neutralize arousal and reduce strain and to concentrate and limit the individual span of attention, (4) body positions or altered states of consciousness are used to facilitate changes in perception, and (5) unusual events are used as triggers to produce or enhance the process of conversion.

In contrast to the situation in which the group provides a new meaning for an individual, in many societies there are persons whose business it is to seek and find new meanings for the group. Cole describes the shaman who goes into a trance state to make a voyage to the place where new insights are found, and the hungan who is possessed by those who provide the insights. The process is a more elaborate version of the process that any individual must go through to gain a new insight into the situation and to make it "present" for other members of the group.

The public drama, as identified by Gusfield, is a third example of the way in which new meanings are developed. In this case the public media, or person of authority, creates an enactment to build up a sense of an orderly world. One illustration is the public presentation of the problem of the "killer-drunk" who ignores the boundaries of prudent living and planning. A second illustration is the case of former U.S. President Nixon, who publicly covered himself with shame after being impeached, an act that helped restore the sense of legitimacy of the presidency as an institution.

PART III

Varieties of Enactment

10

Football Victory Celebrations in America

David A. Snow, Louis A. Zurcher, and Robert Peters

The purpose of this paper is twofold: (1) to contribute empirical data on crowd behavior by describing and analyzing a series of college football victory celebrations: and (2) to apply a dramaturgical analysis to crowd behavior, focusing on interaction rather than on the cognitive or demographic characteristics of the participants. The intent is not to displace existing approaches to the study of the crowd. Rather, it is to complement them, particularly the emergent norm thesis and the gaming or rational calculus perspective.

DATA AND PROCEDURES

On five consecutive Saturday evenings from October 8, 1977 to November 5, 1977, students from The University of Texas and other Austin residents converged on the main street bordering the University and transformed it into an arena for celebrating the victories of the University football team. Data about the celebrations were derived from three sources. Following a team approach to fieldwork, we first observed the celebration *in situ*. One of the authors, who lived within earshot of the celebrations, assumed the

From "Victory celebrations as theater: A dramaturgical approach to crowd behavior" by David A. Snow, Louis A. Zurcher, and Robert Peters, 1981, *Symbolic Interaction, 4* (1), pp. 22–27, 31–36. Reprinted [with footnotes omitted] by permission of JAI Press Inc.

role of a participant observer for each of the episodes. Another author, although attending some of the celebrations, functioned mainly as a detached observer. The participant observer roamed through the different spatial sectors of the celebrations, occasionally hitching a ride on a parading vehicle, and talked with representatives of the different segments of the crowd. He was able to record hundreds of behaviors and gestures and to interview informally several of the participants. The detached observer, functioning primarily as a cross-examiner, critically appraised the fieldnotes and interviewed the participant observer. Each Monday following a celebration the participant observer and the detached observer would meet in a debriefing session and establish a research agenda in the event of another celebration.

As a check on our own observations and fieldnotes, 15 university students, each of whom had participated in the victory crowds, were interviewed in the weeks following the celebrations. We were less interested in the representativeness of the student respondents than we were in how well their recollections corresponded with our own observations.

The third data source consisted of press accounts in the campus and city newspapers. These accounts, including letters to the editors regarding the celebrations, were examined for information about community reaction and for evidence confirming or disconfirming our observations. Although the three data sources yielded no major inconsistencies, it might appear that the data base was thin. We would argue, however, that the data we collected are far better than none, especially in a substantive area rife with theoretical speculation about phenomena that have too infrequently been directly studied.

THE VICTORY CELEBRATIONS

On October 8, 1977, The University of Texas football team unexpectedly defeated its arch-rival, the University of Oklahoma, for the first time in seven years. Immediately following the game's conclusion (4:30 p.m.), many students and other local fans began driving along "the Drag," the section of Guadalupe Street bounding the western edge of the University campus (see Figure 10.1). Even though the game had not been played at "home," by

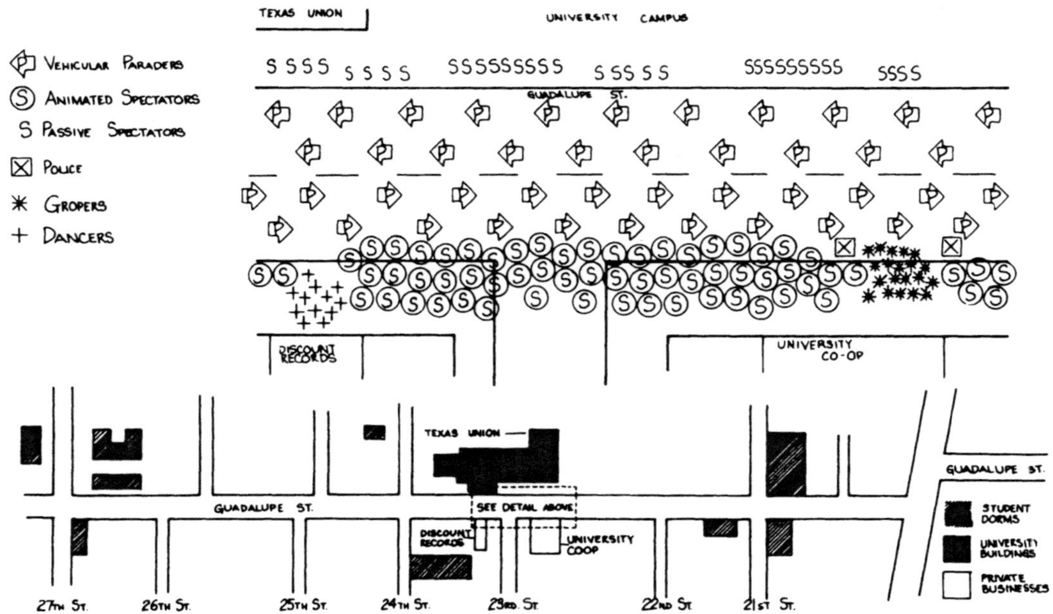

Figure 10.1

Diagram of "The Drag" and location of the six types of participants, 1st celebration, October 8, 1977.

(From David A. Snow, Louis A. Zurcher, and Robert Peters, "Victory celebrations as theater: A dramaturgical approach to crowd behavior," *Symbolic Interaction*, 4 (1), p. 24. Reprinted by permission.)

8:00 p.m. approximately 3,000 people had gathered on the Drag. There was bumper-to-bumper traffic between Nineteenth and Twenty-Sixth Streets (which constitute the northern and southern boundaries of the University campus). The street resounded with the din of honking horns and shouts of "we're No. 1!" The celebration, which was likened to "a big New Year's party" by one participant, lasted until early Sunday morning.

Throughout the evening six types of participants and corresponding behaviors were clearly discernible (see Figure 10.1). The first type consisted of the vehicular paraders or occupants of the motor vehicles who, as the focus of attention, constituted the main performers. A few of the cars had roof-mounted loudspeakers blaring "we're No. 1." All of the vehicles were filled with celebrants who, hanging out of the car windows or sitting on the car roofs, guzzled beer, yelled, flashed the "Hook-em-Horns" sign, and slapped hands with other paraders and spectators who lined the street.

The second group of participants consisted of relatively passive spectators who sat on the cement wall that separates the University campus from the public sidewalk. Periodically a few of these spectators would yell and flash the "Hook-em" sign, but their main activity was viewing.

The third type were the more animated spectators. Congregated mainly on the west side of the Drag immediately north of Twenty-Second Street, these participants actively supported the vehicular paraders by shaking their hands and cheering them on. Immediately behind these spectators was the fourth set of participants. This group consisted of a small number of people who were dancing to the rock music blaring out of a record store.

The fifth type was represented by males who stood across from the Student Union just south of Twenty-Third Street. Whenever a car or pickup [a light van with an open body] approached, they would slap the side and top of the vehicle and attempt to "grope" the female occupants.

The sixth group of participants was comprised of the police scattered along the Drag. Decidedly friendly, the police appeared to function more as supportive viewers than as control agents. Except for keeping the autos within their appropriate lanes and occasionaly asking some of the more animated spectators to move back, the police maintained a low and cordial profile. This was reflected in part by the fact that none of the participants at this first celebration were arrested, even through many of them were in fact breaking the law.

The following Saturday (October 15), Texas' football team came from behind in the final quarter to defeat the University of Arkansas. Moments after the game, fans again converged on the Drag. They began celebrating in a manner similar to the previous week, but with three discernible differences. First, there was a greater number of vehicular paraders. Not only was the traffic backed-up further than the previous week, but there were more celebrants sitting in and on the cars and pickups. Second, females were not being molested by male spectators. Third, not only had the number of spectators increased, but they had become more animated. As before, the police did little to dampen the jovial mood or to stop the celebration, which could still be heard from a mile away at 4:30 Sunday morning.

While Texas was defeating Southern Methodist University on Saturday, October 22, No. 1 ranked University of Michigan was losing to the University of Minnesota. This upset, coupled with Texas' win, meant that Texas would probably become the No. 1 ranked team in the nation. Partly because of this unanticipated turn of events, the ensuing celebration was the largest and most vociferous to date. Honking horns rhythmically pounded out "we're No. 1" while riders waved Texas state flags, shook hands with spectators and tossed cans of beer to those weaving in and out of the bumper-to-bumper traffic which extended 15 blocks in either direction. But most of this activity was not evident until the vehicular paraders entered the area of Guadalupe that had been transformed into an arena for celebration. As paraders entered the "stage," their level of animation increased and the noise became almost deafening. The crowd activity reached its peak in the vicinity of Twenty-Third Street and the Student Union (see Figure 10.1), where the number of spectators was most dense. Again, the police were unobtrusive. Most of the time they stood watching the celebrants, occasionally shaking hands with some of them and flashing the "Hook-em" sign.

Following Texas' defeat of Texas Tech University on Saturday, October 29, fans again converged on the Drag. With bumper-to-bumper traffic extending for 34 blocks by early evening, it appeared as if the celebration would be the wildest to date. The fact that this was the first celebration to follow a home game also suggested a likely increase in intensity. However, the celebration was subdued and constrained in comparison to those previous. There was less physical contact between paraders and spectators. There were fewer celebrants per vehicle. There was less hand-slapping and little rhythmical horn-blowing. The overall volume of noise had decreased.

These changes in the behavior of the the celebrants seemed largely due to a shift in police strategy and demeanor. The number of officers had increased from the previous week's level of approximately 5 per block to a new level of 8 to 10 per block. In addition, the majority of the policemen were now suited in high leather boots and riot helmets. Now, rather than shaking hands and flashing the "Hook-em" sign, the police were concentrating on directing traffic, keeping celebrants off the tops and hoods of cars, and keeping spectators out of the street. In contrast to the earlier celebrations, the police were occasionally arresting lawbreaking celebrants.

Since these changes in police behavior interfered with the celebrating, some of the celebrants later in the evening (11 p.m.) shifted their activity further down the Drag where there were fewer police. Whereas the segment of the Drag directly across from the Student Union had functioned as "center stage," a substitute area was appropriated and redefined for celebration by some of the spectators. Until police reinforcements arrived at the new site, celebrants were once again sitting on car hoods and hanging out of the windows, honking the car horns, walking back and forth between cars, shaking hands, and screaming "we're No. 1."

Texas' defeat of the University of Houston on Saturday, November 5, provided the impetus for another celebration. However, this post-game celebration was even more muted than the previous one. The major categories of actors returned, but their behavior had changed dramatically, as if the script had been rewritten. Though there were at least 1,000 celebrators on the Drag, there was little yelling. There were only scattered horn blowing and few overfilled cars and pickups. The mood was one of caution; the watchword was "Ssshhh." The apparent reason for the change was a significant increase in the number of police assigned to the Drag. Officers were standing every 30 to 40 feet on the center dividing line and on each side of the street. Police were stationed north of Twenty-Sixth Street for the first time since the celebrations had begun. The officers had been instructed (for reasons that will be discussed later) to reduce the overall level of noise. Whenever a horn was blown, the officer who spotted the violator would stop the vehicle or shine his flashlight on the side of the auto and the next policeman would stop the car. As a result of this tactic, the noise was greatly reduced.

Nonetheless, some vehicular paraders, coaxed by the spectators, continued to drive up and down the Drag. Whenever a car horn sounded, spectators in the immediate area would applaud and cheer. If a parader received a citation, the police were booed. Though the encouragement did not lead to an increase in the actual amount of horn blowing, it did help produce an atmosphere conducive to taunting the police. Many paraders would shout "honk, honk" as they passed police: others mockingly would put a finger to their lips in the "Ssshhh" position. In response, one officer commented, "I'd almost rather they did honk. At least there would be something to do." As the evening progressed, it became evident that the interaction between the police and the vehicular paraders had now become the focus of attention.

The following Saturday, November 12, when Texas defeated Texas Christian University, the only actors to appear on the Drag in full force were the police. There was little celebration: traffic was near normal. There were several reasons for the apparent disinterest in celebration. First, although Texas won, the victory was anticipated. Second, the Saturday morning edition of the city newspaper indicated that the police would attempt "to put a damper on any celebration." As on the previous Saturday, there were approximately 10 police per block. Moreover, they were giving a traffic citation to anyone who blew a car horn. This show of force and "crack-down" strategy seemed to intimidate potential celebrants. Only three "honks" were heard and recorded within a 15-minute period between 8 p.m. and 9 p.m. A third countervailing factor was the rumor that "a sniper would be on the Drag" on Saturday evening. Both Friday's edition of the campus newspaper and the Saturday morning edition of the city newspaper reported that the Austin police had received an anonymous letter warning that the writer would "shoot up the Drag Saturday night" in the event of another celebration. Although the police were "pretty satisfied it (was) just a crank," such a threat could not be fully discounted, especially since it stimulated memories of a sniper who in 1967 had terrorized the University of Texas campus. A fourth countervailing factor was the annual sausage festival (Wurstfest) south of Austin. The festival provided an entertainment alternative to the Drag, thereby siphoning many potential celebrants. Finally, it is reasonable to assume that for many of the participants the celebrations were becoming routine and predictable; the novelty had worn off.

After five weeks, the series of victory celebrations had run its course. In the weeks that followed, Texas won its final two regularly scheduled games. Neither was followed by a victory celebration of the kind that had occurred earlier.

ANALYSIS AND DISCUSSION

. . . Most scholars would agree that the victory celebrations on the Drag constituted a series of crowd episodes. On each occasion there was a large number of people in close physical contact within a limited spatial area. There was a common focus of attention. Though some "assembling instructions" (McPhail and Miller, 1973) such as shouts of "to the Drag" were heard after the first celebration, the assemblage and ensuing behaviors were relatively spontaneous and unplanned. The celebrations were neither on the community or university calendars nor were they the product of prior formal organization. This is not to suggest that the celebrations were devoid of organization or patterned behavior. To the contrary, it appeared as if the actions of the different segments of the crowd fit together, as if they were aligned in a complementary fashion. How can that coordination be best explained? How did the lines of action exhibited by the different categories of participants fit together and contribute to the development of the celebrations? Additionally, what accounts for the shift in the behavior of some of the participants and for the change in the character of the celebrations? . . .

We suggest that the character and direction of the victory crowds we observed can be best understood in terms of the interaction among the participants who either functioned as performers and spectators, or alternated between the two categories. We will first consider the performers, and then examine the "proximal spectators" and their relative influence. Since the police functioned as both spectators and performers, their behavior and influence are considered in relation to another audience, the bystanders or "distal spectators."

Task Performers

During the course of the celebrations a variety of activities were readily observable. Wright (1978), who similarly reported considerable behavioral heterogeneity during his first-hand examination of collective encounters, has suggested that these behaviors may be differentiated according to whether they are "task" or "crowd" activities. Crowd activities refer to redundant behaviors seemingly universal to all collective encounters, such as assemblage and milling. Task activities include those behaviors that are particular to and necessary for the attainment of a specific goal or resolution of a specific problem. From a dramaturgical standpoint, we would add that task activities constitute the primary objects of attention, and that those crowd participants engaging in such activities constitute the task performers.

Throughout the celebrations several task performers were clearly observable, such as the vehicular paraders, the "gropers," the dancers, and the police. There was even a group of religious fundamentalists that appeared one evening in an effort to promote their cause and recruit members. What distinguished the various task performers from the spectators is that rather than visually attending to the business of others, they engaged in activities specific to the tasks of celebrating, dancing, molesting women, or promoting Jesus. It was these performances that provided the spectators with something to view.

However, not all of the task performances were equally attended to by the spectators. Indeed it appeared as if all but the vehicular paraders, and later the police, were ignored. Consequently, it is useful to classify task activities according to the amount of attention they receive, and according to their salience to the character of the collective encounter. Those behaviors which are the major focus of attention and which give meaning to the occasion can be regarded as the *main task activity*. Those task performances subordinate to the main task activity constitute side or *subordinate task activities*. Put metaphorically, the major task activity is the main performance. It is on center stage. In contrast, the remaining task activities are side shows, subordinate and often parasitic to the main event. In the victory crowds the vehicular paraders functioned as the main task performers, at least until the fifth celebration when the police and their interaction with the paraders became the focus of attention.

Since the activities of the vehicular paraders were more in keeping with the spirit of the occasion, it is understandable why they, rather than the other task performances, were the focus of attention. But why did the paraders keep performing? Why was the performance confined to a specific spatial area? What defined "the stage?" What accounted not only for alteration in the behavior of the vehicular paraders, but also for the shift in orientation of the police? To answer these questions we must consider the spectators in detail.

Proximal Spectators

By proximal spectators we mean those physically co-present participants who function primarily as viewers. Whether voluntary or involuntary, animated or passive, their major activity consisted of watching the paraders celebrate.

Turner and Killian (1972:93–94) have noted that spectators constitute an important element of the crowd because they swell its ranks and thereby create the impression of solidarity. Our observations suggest that spectators function not only in this supportive manner, but they also define the character of the activity they observe. In some instances, spectators offered verbal or gestural support for a new line of activity exhibited by innovative paraders. In other instances spectators called for specific lines of action. Those "calls" included thrusting out an open palm in order "to get five" from the passing paraders, yelling for the performers to ignore the police, and urging the performers to get on with "the show." When the police began to curtail the noise, for example, groups of spectators would call for the paraders to honk their horns. Rather than only responding to the main task performance and accepting the activity as given, the more animated spectators attempted to influence the character of the celebration.

The presence of spectators also functioned to determine the level of animation and noise produced by the vehicular paraders. Whenever spectators were absent, the paraders were relatively quiet and motionless. The only apparent activity occurred when a car approached from the opposite direction and blew its horn. However, as the vehicles approached an area where spectators were present, the paraders would "go into play"; that is, they would begin to yell, blow their horns, hang out the window, and flash the "Hook-em-Horns" sign. This interactional pattern was so dominant that paraders would cease to celebrate once out of view of the spectators. Then, after turning their cars around and getting back on the Drag, the paraders would "turn on" or "come into play" once again.

The influence of the presence of spectators was demonstrated even more dramatically during the fourth celebration when many of the spectators moved north of the Drag, redefining the portion of Guadalupe between Twenty-Ninth and Thirty-First Street as the "new stage." The vehicular paraders driving into that area went into "play," performing as they had earlier when the Drag was defined as the arena for celebration.

These observations indicate that the audience more than the main task performers defined the stage or area in which the celebrations were conducted. It is thus reasonable to suggest that in this particular series of crowd episodes the audience, rather than being merely supportive or facilitative, was structurally essential. Simply put: no audience, no victory celebrations.

Social Control Agents and Distal Spectators

Another group of actors which comprised part of the crowd and influenced the course and character of the celebrations were the police. We emphasized earlier that the character of the fourth celebration was strikingly different from those previous. Not only was there a discernible change in the behavior of the vehicular paraders, who had become more constrained, but there was a corresponding shift in the orientation of the police. Our observations suggest that the alteration in the activity of the main task performers was largely due to the change in the demeanor of the police.

Initially the police viewed the celebrations as good clean fun. They maintained a low profile, alternating between being supportive spectators and subordinate task performers. As one of the commanding officers commented after the first celebrations:

> This crowd was in a partying mood . . . not a trouble-making mood. They were not intent on tearing up anything. Far be it from us to interfere with a good party.

In the midst of the third celebration another officer, who stood on the sidewalk watching the "party," similarly commented that "there's not much else we can do. They're just having fun." There were other lines of action that might have been pursued, but the police had adopted a policy of nonintervention. In the middle of the week prior to the fourth celebration a public information officer confessed that the police had been "rather lenient the last three weeks," adding that "we have not put some people in jail that we could have." However, shortly after the fourth celebration began it was clear that the police had redefined the crowd activity as something other than "fun." Twice as many officers were assigned to the Drag, and they were wearing riot helmets and high boots. They were also less congenial and more task oriented. Instead of standing on the sidelines and flashing the "Hook-em-Horns" sign, they were now stopping the paraders. They directed people to remain in their cars and to refrain from blowing their car horns. They issued warnings and citations. Finally, and most significantly, by the end of the evening the police had arrested several celebrants.

In attempting to control the proceedings, the police had become a focus of attention for both the vehicular paraders and the proximal spectators. They were competing with the vehicular paraders for control of "center stage," while simultaneously neutralizing the influence of the animated spectators. What was previously an occasion condoned or tolerated by the police had been redefined as an occasion that needed to be controlled and diffused. What transpired between the third and fourth celebrations to account for the change?

The answer to this question requires consideration of another audience that Turner and Killian (1972:238–40) have termed a "bystander public." The concept denotes a diffuse collectivity that emerges when prolonged crowd behavior is perceived as a threat to personal routines and public order. According to Turner and Killian (1972:238), bystanders have no particular stake in the demonstration, celebration, or conflict that constitutes an object of attention. Rather, they are concerned with the "restoration of order and the elimination of danger and inconvenience," whether real or anticipated. Since our observations indicate that each celebration prompted the emergence of bystander spectators, and that their responses were not all unfavorable, we find it necessary to broaden the conceptualization. Accordingly, we define a bystander public or audience as a diffuse collectivity of distal spectators who indirectly monitor an instance of crowd behavior and respond to it, either favorably or unfavorably, by registering their respective views with the media, the press, and/or with community officials. Although not directly involved in the crowd attended to, distal spectators can affect its career and outcome by indirectly influencing one or more groups of participants.

Our research indicates that the emergence of distal spectators did indeed influence the behavior of the police in particular and the character of the celebrations in general. This observation is suggested by the data derived from a content analysis of all celebration-related articles, editorials, and letters-to-the-editors appearing in the *Austin American Statesman* and the University *Daily Texan* from the day after the first celebration to seven days following the last regularly scheduled game. As indicated in Figure 10.2, which summarizes the findings, it was not until the week following the third celebration that distal spectators began to clamor for the control and dissolution of the celebrations. Since the change in police demeanor and strategy occurred during the following (fourth) celebration, we argue that the shift was largely attributable to the emergence of distal spectators who viewed the celebrations negatively, publicly calling for the restoration of order.

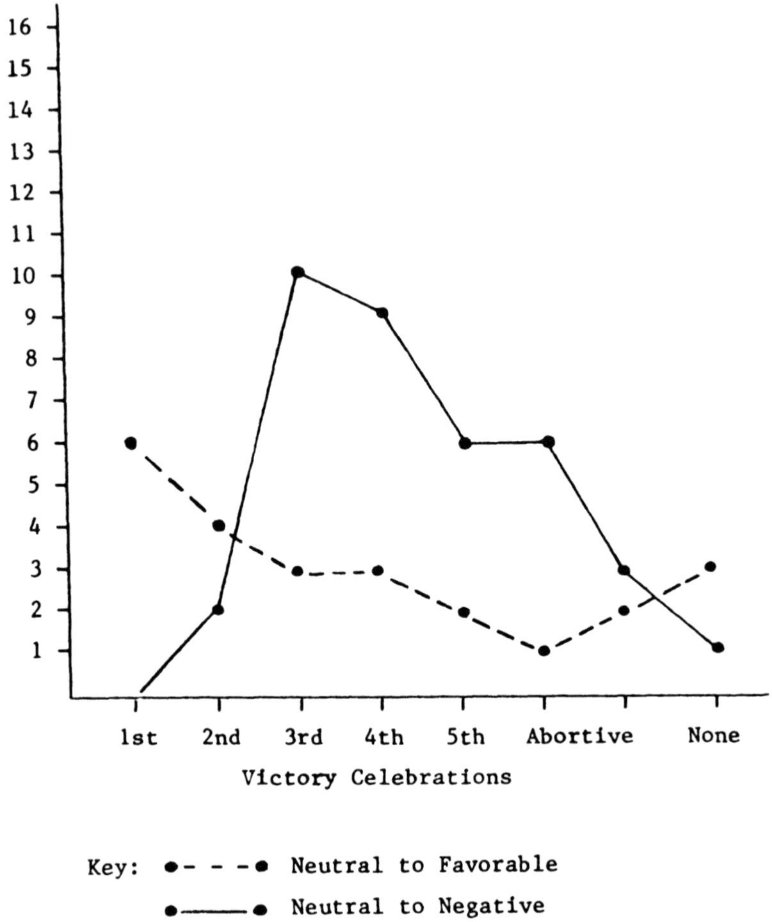

Figure 10.2
Number of articles and editorials responding favorably or negatively to the celebrations.

(From David A. Snow, Louis A. Zurcher, and Robert Peters, "Victory celebrations as theater: A dramaturgical approach to crowd behavior," *Symbolic Interaction*, 4 (1), p. 35. Reprinted by permission.)

Prior to the third celebration, distal spectators, including the press, responded favorably to the victory crowds. Following the first celebration, for example, the city newspaper referred to the celebration as "Happy Days"; and a letter to the editor encouraged celebrants to "Keep (their) Horns High." The following week such terms as "ecstasy" and "joy" were still being used to describe the celebrations. However, by the end of the week following the third celebration it was clear that either there had been a change in attitude among distal spectators or that a less congenial group of distal spectators had emerged. Whatever the case, not only had the celebrations become more of a community issue, as evidenced by the increase in the number of newspaper accounts devoted to them (see Figure 10.2), but the celebrations were now being described as "unruly," "childish," "drunken sprees," "expensive," and "public disturbances." In response to the negative public reaction, local officials urged the celebrants to "cool it." On the Thursday following the third celebration, the city mayor issued a press release in which she called on police to "clamp down" on the celebrants whose actions "would harm any citizen, damage property or abuse any individual's rights." In a letter appearing in the campus newspaper on the same day, a university official called on "students to exercise . . . maturity and good judgment," and warned that continued celebration would make "large numbers of students subject to traffic citations, arrests, and prosecution."

In light of the distal spectators' redefinition of the celebrations as "disturbances," and their demand for celebrant restraint and police vigilance, the change in police behavior is understandable. Although this change altered the character of the fourth celebration, distal spectators continued to pressure public officials to control the "fanatics" and put an end to the "curse." The police thus maintained their "show-of-force" and "crack-down" strategy. As a result, the fifth celebration was the most subdued to date. In the weeks that followed, the police were the only group of actors to appear in significant presence. By the time the last regularly scheduled game was completed, it was clear that the police had become the main task performers. The Drag was once again a street rather than an arena for celebration. As one supportive distal spectator commented, "the spectacle wasn't loyal Texas fans waving their horns, but the 80 or so cops who lined the Drag."

In summary, our observations suggest that just as the activity of the vehicular paraders was influenced by the proximal spectators, including the police, so the police activity, and ultimately the character of the celebrations, was influenced by the emergence of distal spectators calling for the restoration of order.

[*Summary by A. Paul Hare:* Snow, Zurcher, and Peters present observations on five university football victory celebrations that took place on the main street of a university town in the United States. They note six types of roles being played by sets of persons: vehicular paraders, animated spectators, passive spectators, police, gropers (males who would attempt to "grope" the female occupants of passing cars), and dancers (persons dancing to rock music from a record store).

They divide the performing groups into those who were the major focus of attention, that is, held center stage (the vehicular paraders), and those who were subordinate to the main event (gropers and dancers). For the first four celebrations the vehicular paraders were the focus of attention, and for the fifth the interaction between police and paraders became the focus.

Proximal spectators, whether voluntary or involuntary, active or passive, both swelled the ranks of the crowd and defined the character of the activity by verbal or gestural support for new lines of activity. The course of events was also significantly altered by the definition of the situation given by the police. At first the police defined the crowd activity as fun. Later they decided that the crowd needed to be controlled and defused. The behavior of the police was influenced by the opinions of the distal spectators who registered their views with the media and community officials. They saw the celebrations as a threat to personal routines and public order.

The observations illustrate the importance of identifying the ideas that form a focus of attention for smaller groups of actors within a large group. Also they emphasize the importance of the part played by the audience in defining the situation for the active participants. Additional accounts of football and other sports events from a dramaturgical perspective are given by Deegan and Stein (1978), Keenan (1975), Marsh, Rosser, and Harré (1978), Porter (1977), and Zurcher (1982).]

11

Protest Demonstration in South Africa

A. Paul Hare

South Africa has a long history of protest demonstrations. Some that received world-wide attention were those organized by Gandhi in the early 1900s, during which he developed most of his techniques for nonviolent action, and the 1976 student demonstrations, especially in SOWETO, that revived mass protest after a period of relative quiet since the 1960s. The tragic incident at the police station in the black township of Sharpeville in 1960, when police fired at a large crowd of blacks killing 69 persons and wounding many others, had led many people to believe that mass protest had been contained and would not appear again. This chapter provides an analysis of the incident from a dramaturgical perspective by considering the way it was staged, the images that police and crowd held of each other, and the amount of creativity evident in the actions of different protagonists and segments of the crowd during the event.

To depict the images the field diagram developed by Bales (Bales and Cohen, 1979) is used with the four dimensions of interpersonal behavior: upward–downward, positive–negative, serious–expressive, and conforming–anticonforming (see Table 11.1). In the field diagram the positive–negative dimension is represented on the horizontal axis, and the serious–expressive dimension on the vertical axis. The upward–downward dimension is represented by the size of the circle indicating the location of an image, with smaller circles representing downward (submissive) images and larger circles representing upward (dominant) images. The extent

Table 11.1
Interaction Process Analysis, Four Dimensions

I. Upward vs. downward	
Upward:	Assuming autocratic control or seeking status in the group by making direct suggestions or by giving opinions that serve to guide group activity. (Also measured by total talking rate.)
Downward:	Showing dependence by asking for help, showing anxiety, shame and guilt, or frustration, laughing at the jokes of a dominant person.
II. Positive vs. negative	
Positive:	Seeming friendly by showing affection, agreement, or by asking for information or opinion in an encouraging way.
Negative:	Seeming unfriendly by disagreeing, showing antagonism, or diffuse aggression.
III. Serious vs. expressive	
Serious:	Giving information or opinions that indicate serious involvement in the task. Routine agreement.
Expressive:	Giving support to others regardless of task performance or showing tension release through joking or other evidence of flight from the task.
IV. Conforming vs. anticonforming	
Conforming:	Seeking to be guided by the group norms by asking for information or suggestions. Making jokes or dramatic statements that reveal the basic nature of the group.
Anticonforming:	Showing tension that indicates withdrawal from the field. Describing fantasies that reveal individual goals rather than group goals. Resisting pressure to conform.

Source: Reprinted with permission of publisher from: Hare, A. P. Four dimensions of interpersonal behavior. *Psychological Reports*, 1972, 30, 499–512. Fig. 10.

to which the image is anticonforming or conforming is represented by the letter "C" with a number from 1 to 7, where 1 is very anticonforming and 7 is very conforming.

For levels of creativity, a category system is used based on five distinctions made by Taylor (1975:305–8) for identifying creative contributions to a whole society. Taylor's labels for the five categories are used, but the content is adapted to reflect the kinds of activity that appear in small-group problem solving and negotiations (Hare and Naveh, 1986:245–46). (See Table 11.2.) For an

Table 11.2
Categories of Creativity

1. *Expressive*—spontaneous contributions that indicate that a person is warming up for the *task*. Also work that is personally need-oriented and unrelated to group work. Also suggestions that allow a group to bypass a problem without actually solving it.
2. *Technical*—contributions or solution that involve skill and a new level of proficiency. Also work that is maintaining and routine in character. Also providing a standard or "textbook" solution to a problem.
3. *Inventive*—ingenuity with materials, providing combinations to solve old problems in new ways. Also suggesting alternative methods for solving a problem or clarifying already established plans. Also providing solutions that involve "trade-offs," so that each party receives some gain.
4. *Innovative*—basic principles are understood so that older theories can be extended to cover new areas. Also active problem solving by introducing unusual points of view. Also "extending the margins" of concepts to fit new situations.
5. *Emergenitive*—involves the most abstract ideational principles or assumptions underlying a body of art or science. Also work that is highly insightful and integrative. It often interprets what has been going on in the group and brings together in a meaningful way a series of experiences. Also suggestions that allow a group to reach consensus through a new definition of the situation.

Source: From "Conformity and creativity: Camp David, 1978" by A. Paul Hare and David Naveh, 1986, *Small Group Behavior,* 17 (3), 243–68. Reprinted by permission of Sage Publications, Inc.

instance of collective behavior such as that at Sharpeville, category 1 includes self-oriented behavior that is not related to group work, category 2 is behavior that is routine, category 3 is for active engagement in the activity, category 4 represents a higher level of involvement, and category 5 is reserved for acts that bring new meaning to the situation. In a case of collective behavior these are the acts that set the dominant image or theme.

The description of the incident at Sharpeville and the dramaturgical analysis that follows are reproduced from *Social Interaction as Drama* (Hare, 1985:63–72). The account of events that is used for analysis is an official report of a Commission appointed by the South African Government. Although other accounts by persons supporting the black protestors were consulted (i.e. Reeves, 1960), the account of the Commission proved to be the most complete by providing verbatim records of testimony. The analysis was done during my period of residence in South Africa from 1973 through 1982, and an earlier version was used as background for discussions with members of the government and the black community in an attempt to alert both sides to the tragic effects that can follow at least partly from *conflicting perceptions* of the definition of a situation. Readers who are interested in some of the activities of those of us concerned with nonviolent action in South Africa during the period 1977–1981 will find a number of accounts in *The Struggle for Democracy in South Africa: Conflict and Conflict Resolution* (Hare, 1983).

SHARPEVILLE, 1960*

For the analysis of any incident of conflict or conflict resolution, it is best if the persons recording the event are familiar with the theoretical categories that will be used in the analysis. When this is the case, they can record relevant information that may well be overlooked by an observer with a more general orientation.

*From *Social Interaction as Drama: Applications from Conflict Resolution* by A. Paul Hare, 1985, Beverly Hills, CA: Sage Publications. Pp. 63–71. Reprinted by permission of Sage Publications, Inc.

However, in the case of the incident at the Sharpeville police station on Monday, March 21, 1960, there is no evidence that any social scientist was present, least of all one using a "dramaturgical perspective." However, Judge Wessels, who was appointed as a commission to investigate and report on these events, provided a report of some 200 pages that gives the background of the occurrences as well as an hour-by-hour account of the activities during the morning and early afternoon (Wessels, 1960). The references to the Commission report are to paragraph numbers rather than page numbers, because I was using an English translation of the official report (that was only issued in Afrikaans) and the page numbers may not be the same.

The events at Sharpeville were only one part of a nationwide protest organized by members of the Pan Africanist Congress in the hope that if a sufficient number of persons without passes would present themselves for arrest at police stations then the ensuing work stoppage would signal the beginning of a major protest on the part of blacks. The leaders of the P.A.C. hoped that in three-years' time the country would be turned over to them. During the weekend before March 21, and in the early hours of that Monday morning, there had been confrontations between police and groups of black protestors. Some of these confrontations had been violent, and large crowds had gathered, especially on Seeiso Street, not far from the Sharpeville police station. During the night, the telephone lines to the police station had been cut, so that there was no direct communication with police at the station about the conditions there until police vehicles with radios arrived later in the day. Thus, unfortunately for the persons who eventually gathered in the crowd at the Sharpeville police station, impressions were formed about their behavior by some of the key police officers that were based on information about conflicts that had occurred at other locations earlier in the day.

The main activity began at the Sharpeville police station at 8:00 a.m. when Tsolo, a 20-year-old leader of the P.A.C., arrived with a group of about 40 blacks and asked that they be arrested because they were not carrying passes. Sergeant Nkosi said that he could not arrest anyone and that they must wait for one of the white officers to arrive. At 9:00 a.m., Head Constable Heyl arrived and took over command. This followed the custom of the police that whenever an officer of higher rank arrived on the scene, he would be given command. As a result, the command at the Sharpeville police station changed four times during the morning and early afternoon, about every hour or hour-and-a-half, and no officer in charge was able to form a direct impression of the mood of the crowd over the whole period.

When Head Constable Heyl arrived, Tsolo again asked that his group be arrested. He was told to make his representations to the government and not to the police. By this time, the crowd around the police station was estimated to be more than 3,000 persons. At 10:30 a.m., Lt. Visser (a member of the detective branch) took over command. Tsolo again asked to be locked up. After his conversations with Lt. Visser the impression was given to the crowd that some important official would come to speak to them at 2.00 p.m. From then on, many members of the crowd were simply waiting or watching the events unfold as airplanes buzzed the area in an attempt to disperse the crowd, but only succeeding in attracting more interest. From time to time, various groups of police reinforcements with vehicles arrived and passed through the crowd and into the police station through the front double gage (see Figure 11.1). At 11.30 a.m., a group of police took up a position outside the fence surrounding the police station at the entrance of Zwane Street. Although they observed the shooting that took place later, they did not take part in it. During this period, Tsolo and two other leaders were able to control the crowd when they were asked by police to do so (Wessels: para. 183). By this time, a group of curious onlookers had formed along the front section of the fence. On occasion, the fence was bent inward as they pressed forward to see the latest arrivals of police.

At 11.20 a.m., Captain Theron arrived with more police and took over command. He regarded the position as serious and decided to disperse the crowd. He radioed for reinforcements (Wessels: para. 191). About this time, Tsolo had gone off for something to eat. Twelve bottles of cool drink were brought to the police by members of the crowd. The police, who regarded the gift as a taunt, asked that the bottles be removed (Wessels: para. 192). By 1:00 p.m., more security police and three armored cars had arrived, bringing the total number of armored cars inside the fence to four (Wessels: para. 193). A group of youths just outside the gate

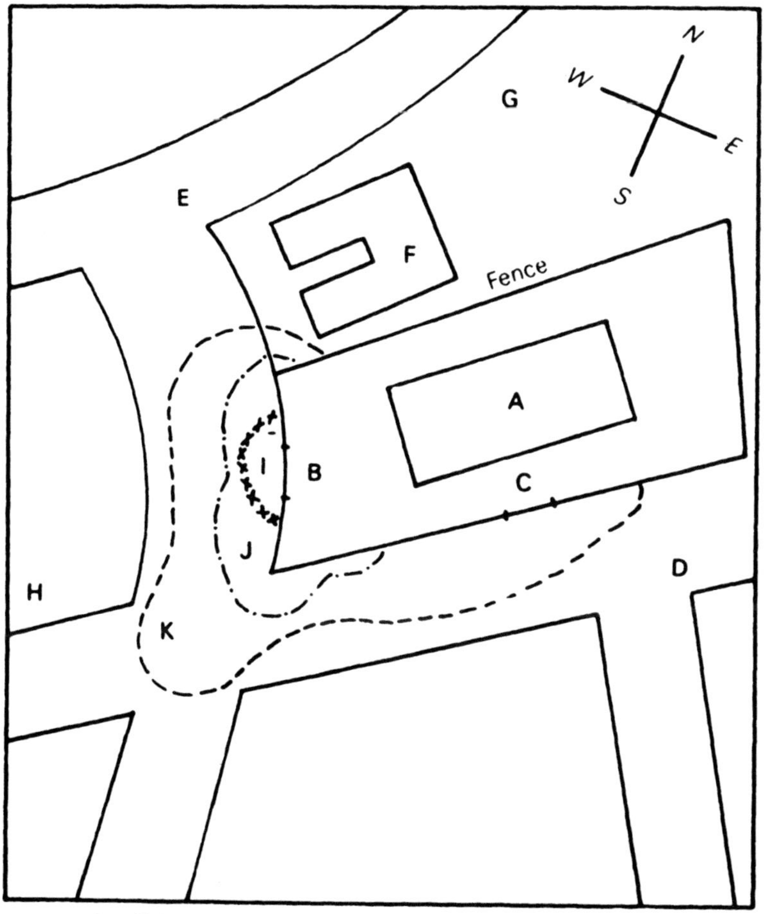

A	Police station	G	North field
B	Main entrance	H	Clinic
C	Side entrance	I	Hostile youths
D	Zwane Street	J	Curious onlookers
E	Seeiso Street	K	Main crowd
F	Cafes and shops		

Figure 11.1
Sharpeville police station and position of crowd.

(From A. Paul Hare, *Social Interaction as Drama: Applications from Conflict Resolution*, p. 66. Copyright © 1985 by Sage Publications, Inc. Reprinted by permission of Sage Publications, Inc.)

at the front of the police station taunted and threatened the police (Wessels: para. 195).

At 1:00 p.m., Lt. Colonel Spengler, of the Security Branch, had arrived. He decided that it might have a beneficial effect on the crowd if he took their leaders inside the police station. So he took Tsolo inside to question him and kept him there (Wessels: para. 197).

Between 1:10 and 1:20 p.m., Lt. Colonel Pienaar drove through the crowd to take command. As he approached the gate, some people struck his car with sticks and he urged his driver to speed through (Wessels: para. 202). Before his arrival, he had been briefed by Major van Zyl about some of the conflicts that had occurred earlier in the day at other locations where there had been violence and attempts to disperse the crowd. Unfortunately, "it is quite clear that Pienaar was under the impression that the attempt to disperse the crowd had taken place at the police station" (Wessels: para. 201). Lt. Col. Pienaar's emotional state at the time is indicated in his statement to the Commission (Wessels: para. 204):

> When I landed inside that yard that morning, from all I had seen and been told and what I had personally experienced, I was satisfied that the mob was ready for anything. The mob was in a frenzied state and I feared an attack on the police at any moment.

In contrast to Lt. Col. Pienaar's impression, the Commission found "no acceptable evidence of any common purpose to attack the police" and the fact that Lt. Col. Spengler considered it safe to open the double gate to take some of the leaders to the police station shows that the members of the Security Branch were not expecting an immediate attack (Wessels: para. 225).

However, Lt. Col. Pienaar's definition of the situation prevailed. As he testified to the Commission (Wessels: para. 229):

> I have had 36 years of service and I have dealt with many mobs. I know what the psychology of a mob is. They have no conscience, are capable of any rash act, and when I landed in the yard, there, my first concern was to muster the police and to form them up in readiness for any possible attack that might come.

Lt. Col. Pienaar then ordered 70 policemen to line up about 7 or 8 paces from the fence facing the crowd in front of the police station. He gave the order to load five rounds.

After the police had been lined up, Lt. Col. Spengler went outside the double gate with the intention of detaining a man in a red shirt who was making a lot of noise. This man did not come in but another man came forward and said that he wished to surrender himself (Wessels: para. 242). There was some sort of brief struggle, some members of the crowd appeared to be coming through the open gate, and the police began to fire although no order had been given. At first, in the confusion, some members of the crowd in the back continued to press forward to see, but within seconds most had turned and started to run away. The police firing probably lasted no more than 20–30 seconds (Wessels: para. 283) before Lt. Col. Pienaar and other officers were able to bring it under control by jumping in front of the policemen, shouting "stop" and waving their hands (Wessels: para. 284). The time was now 1:40 p.m.

There were 130 white and 77 black policemen inside the fence. Another 29 white and 62 black policement were outside the fence. They were ordered not to fire. By the time the shooting stopped, 75 policemen had fired about 700 shots killing 69 and wounding 180 members of the crowd (Wessels: para. 81). About 70% of those killed or wounded had been shot in the back (Wessels: para. 269). It took about one hour to remove the dead and injured (Wessels: para. 310). Judge Wessels (para. 311) concluded that "nothing of note happened later in the day."

A Dramaturgical Analysis of the Events at Sharpeville

For the dramaturgical analysis of an event, two types of diagrams are useful. One is a variation of the "field diagram" proposed by Bales that indicates the relative positions of the actors or images in the four-dimensional space (upward–downward, positive–negative, serious–expressive, and conforming–anticonforming (see Figure 11.2). The other diagram depicts the variations over time in the amount of involvement and creativity of the main individual and group theme carriers during the course of the action (see Figure 11.3).

Depending upon the amount of detail one wishes to record, one might draw field diagrams to indicate the position of actors or images as during each "scene" or "act" in the course of the development of the action. However, in the case of Sharpeville, one field diagram may suffice to indicate the positions of the images that crowd members and police had of themselves and each other at the time the police fired. According to the testimony before the Commission, members of the crowd suggested that although songs were sung and slogans shouted "the crowd was good-humoured throughout." Whereas in the police view "those present at the police station had already been involved earlier in the day in incidents where violence was used both against and by the police; that the feelings of the crowd at the police station gradually became charged through incitement by the leaders until breaking point was reached when at about 1:40 p.m. they started to attack the police and that the police were then obliged to shoot in order to ward off the attack" (Wessels: para. 82).

In Figure 11.2, the images held by members of the crowd are indicated by dashed circles. They see themselves as active (upward) but not too dominant, positive, expressive, and conforming (waiting for someone to speak to them). The images held by members of the police are indicated by the two circles in the upper lefthand corner. The police see the crowd as violent (upward and negative), serious, and anticonforming. In order to control the crowd, the police felt it was necessary to be even more upward, negative, serious, and conforming, in order to drive them back. Unfortunately for the members of the crowd, the events in other areas on the previous night and morning, where some of the police had been on duty, served to remind them of the violence that had occurred at Cato Manor (Wessels: para. 211). There, on January 24, 1960, four white and five black policemen had been murdered by members of a drunken crowd during a weekend liquor raid by the police (Ladlau, 1975:92–97).

A diagram depicting the variations over time of the involvement and creativity of the main theme carriers is given in Figure 11.3. At the left of the diagram is a scale representing the levels of involvement (from 0 to 5) as they are coded according to the previously defined categories for involvement/creativity. At the bottom of the figure is a time line marking each hour and half hour

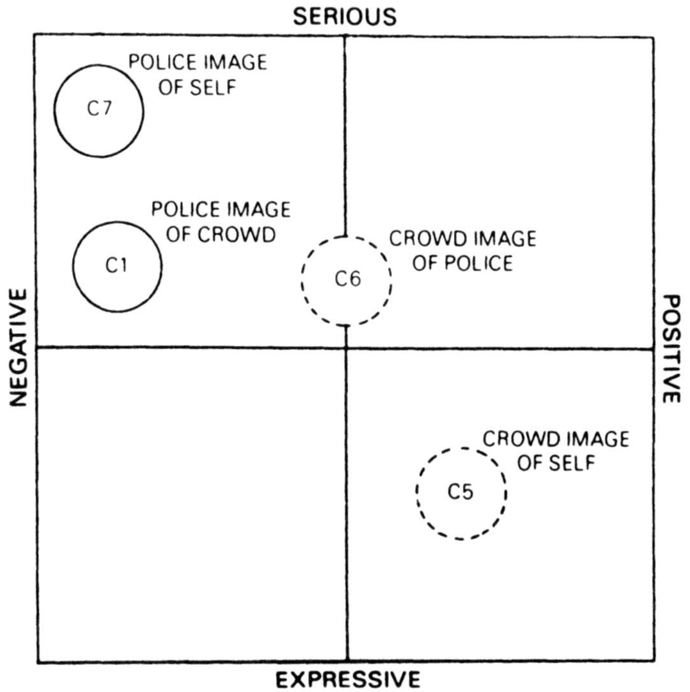

Figure 11.2
Field diagram of images held by crowd and police at Sharpeville.

(From A. Paul Hare, *Social Interaction as Drama: Applications from Conflict Resolution*, p. 69. Copyright © 1985 by Sage Publications, Inc. Reprinted by permission of Sage Publications, Inc.)

from 8:00 a.m. until 2:00 p.m. on Monday, March 21, 1960. The times that the different police officers took command and the time the shooting started is also indicated. The action begins at 8:00 a.m. with Tsolo and the group of about 40 blacks asking to be put in prison. Their initiative (coded as level 5) defined the initial situation at the police station to which Sgt. Nkosi responded. The creativity of Tsolo and his group drops and then rises briefly as they repeat their request to Head Constable Heyl at 9:00 a.m., and later to Lt. Visser. After 10:30, we do not hear about Tsolo's group again.

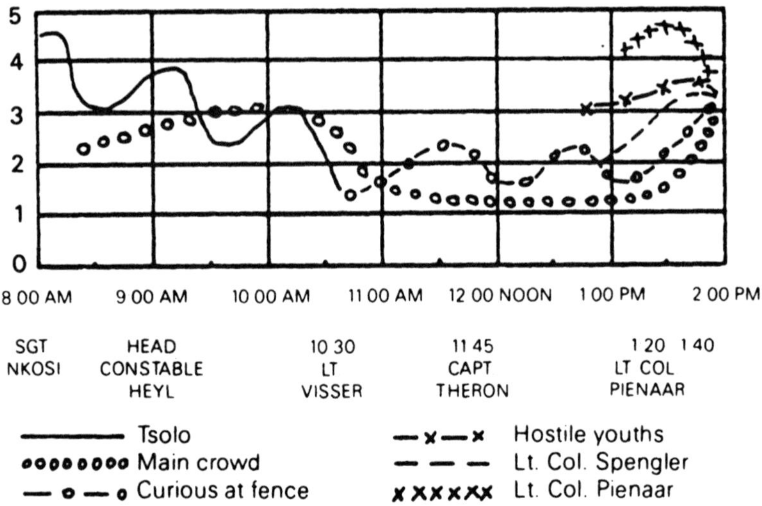

Figure 11.3
Involvement and creativity of theme carriers at Sharpeville police station.
(From A. Paul Hare, *Social Interaction as Drama: Applications from Conflict Resolution*, p. 70. Copyright © 1985 by Sage Publications, Inc. Reprinted by permission of Sage Publications, Inc.)

The involvement of the main crowd (indicated by small circles) begins at about level 2 as they gather to see what is happening. Their level of involvement rises to about level 3 at about 10:30 a.m. when they accept the definition of the situation that someone important will come to speak to them about 2:00 p.m. in the afternoon. They then settle down to wait until 1:40 p.m. when they suddenly discover that they are under attack and flee. Within the main crowd, two smaller segments can be identified. One group consists of the curious onlookers (graph indicated by circles and dashes) who press against the fence from time to time when new police arrive or when Lt. Col. Spengler goes outside the fence to detain someone. The other group contains the hostile youths (graph indicated by crosses and dashes) who gather near the fence and taunt the police. It is the action of these two smaller segments of the crowd that make the major contribution to the image that the police form of the whole crowd, as it is the pressure from the curious at the fence and the stones thrown by the hostile youth that set off the police firing.

However, it is clear that the major theme carrier at the event was Lt. Col. Pienaar who arrived on the scene already convinved that he had only one course of action that might avoid a "blood bath." Without even taking time to order the crowd to disperse he lined up his men and ordered them to load their guns. Thus when Lt. Col. Spengler decided to go outside the gate to detain the last leader, he set in motion a fast-moving sequence of action and reaction that served to convince the other police that their definition of the situation was correct. A few seconds after 1:40 p.m. the creativity on the part of all the actors fell away abruptly, on the police side there was "apparently a feeling of despondency about what had happened" (Wessels: para. 306).

For a single case, such as Sharpeville, one of the main values of using any theory, in this instance a dramaturgical perspective, is that the analyst is forced to consider systematically how the various aspects of the action fit together in terms of the theory. . . .

[*Summary by A. Paul Hare:* The occurrence at the police station in the black township of Sharpeville in South Africa in 1960 is analyzed by considering the staging, the images that the police and crowd held of each other, and the amount of creativity evident in the actions of the different protagonists and segments of the crowd during the event.

Members of the crowd described themselves as "good-humored" throughout the demonstration while they waited for someone to come from Johannesburg to speak to them (an image that is slightly upward, positive, expressive, and conforming). However the police saw the crowd as violent (upward and negative), serious, and anticonforming. Although the crowd did not see the police as threatening, as the police stood around inside the fence awaiting orders, the police conluded that in order to control the crowd, a display of upward, negative, serious, and conforming behavior was necessary.

From the analysis of the levels of creativity of the various protagonists and segments of the crowd over the 5 hour and 40 minute period during which the event took place, we see that the initial defintion of the situation was given by the leader of a group of black men who wished to turn in their passes. As the morning wore on, this group had less influence on the activity, especially after the leader was taken inside the police station. In the early afternoon the group of curious persons at the fence and the group of hostile youths at the gate became more active as more police arrived. An officer of the police Security Branch also took the initiative as he arrested some of the most active members of the crowd. However, it was the definition of the situation brought by the ranking officer of the police when he took over about 30 minutes before the police opened fire on the crowd that had the major effect on the behavior of all present. Once he had set the stage by lining up the police with loaded weapons facing the crowd, a fast-moving sequence of action and reaction was set in motion that resulted in the deaths of 69 members of the crowd and the wounding of 180 others.]

12

Departures and Arrivals in Sri Lanka

R. S. Perinbanayagam

THEORY OF GOOD AND EVIL

The "theory" that is dramatized in ritual and attitude in Jaffna, a homogeneous Hindu-Tamil community in Sri Lanka, is that concerning good and evil. Anything and everything that can be defined as life-giving, fruitful, and bountiful is defined as "good" and anything that suggests life-denial, death, decay, and lameness is "evil." Like all Hundu society, Jaffna too derives its meaning from an essentially agriculture-based society characterized by an economy of scarcity.

To be fruitful and multiply was a serious message to most populations of the world until modern times. Neither medicine nor environmental sciences were able to control diseases and pestilence, thus making replenishment of the stock a constant goal. Hence the people of the world lived in the greatest anxiety and turmoil about being fruitful and connected these anxieties into significant conceptions about the nature of the world: fruitfulness meant good (and good meant fruitfulness) and barrenness meant evil (and vice versa). Such a theory was extended from crops, plants and bees to people as well, and barrenness of all kinds was viewed with foreboding. The upshot of such an experience of nature was to

From "Dramas of structure, theory and performance" by R. S. Perinbanayagam, 1981, *Anthropological Quarterly*, 54 (1), 36–43 (extract includes pages 37–41). Reprinted [with minor agreed changes and with footnotes omitted] by permission.

classify objects in nature as portending or signifying good (life) and evil (death) and using such objects for the organization of social action and the enunciation of dramas. We shall examine here, in particular, the dramas associated with ceremonies of arrival and departure, and those enactments associated with barrenness and fruitfulness. The best way to examine such ceremonies is to view them as *situational dramas* in the sense in which Erving Goffman has approached the analysis of social life.

If situations have organic properties, as Goffman (1964:133) describes them, there is no need to restrict them to any one society. The *sui generis* nature of a social situation does not derive from any cultural peculiarity of society, but from the constitution of the structure of situations. Social situations, by nature, are the occasions in which an individual proposes, initiates, executes and consummates an act. They are, to use Goffman's imagery once again, the moments that have their men who undertake the relevant acts: Not then people and their moments; rather moments and their people" (Goffman 1967:3). These acts that are undertaken *on* these occasions or *in* these moments are indubitably social acts, in the sense in which Mead (1934) defined social acts: they involve the cooperative creation of acts that involve, at least minimally, the incorporation of others—their attitudes, interests, intentions and feelings. Such an approach to the analyses of social situations and social acts enables one to examine the significance of omens, their structure and bearing on the definition of situations and the prosecution of social acts.

DRAMAS OF DEPARTURE

One of the expectations that the various actors have of each other is that they perform their social acts with a certain modicum of ease and control and poise. A loss of any of these factors creates strain in the interaction and may lead to embarrassment (Gross and Stone, 1964; Goffman, 1956). It can even lead to the disruption of relationships and forestall the emergence of relationships.

In the course of life, an actor has to engage often in the social act known as departure. While departures can be routine events of all lives, some are fraught with importance to the actors themselves and to their families. Hence a departure has to be properly staged.

Those that are not routine departures are usually undertaken for tasks of some importance to the person and the family. Such situations have a potential for creating anxiety insofar as they contain an element of uncertainty and encompass a possibility that something untoward or unexpected might happen. Because of their potential, departures are watched closely and undertaken circumspectly. One result of such careful watching and circumspection is the interpretation of various events as signals of coming sorrow and disappointment or joy.

In departing, then, for an enterprise of some moment, the actor, as well as any co-actors, must conduct themselves according to a presumptive sense of orderly self presentation. It is assumed that just as there is an order in the cosmos, there is also an order in situations; if the order is upset, it *must* mean something. Such an upsetting would be deemed to have occurred if (a) the one departing stumbles, sneezes, falters, slips or for that matter falls at the point of leaving the house; (b) someone else sneezes, calls after him or interferes with his leaving in any way; or (c) an untoward sound intrudes on the scene—the chirping of the ubiquitous house gecko, the howling of a dog, the wailing sound of funerals, etc. If none of these "interruptions" (*Thadai*, as they are called in Tamil) occur, the action proceeds as intended—unless of course a bad omen is encountered at the next stage.

What would be done if any of these "interruptions" did occur? It is assumed by the actors that actions leading to fruition are achieved in an even and uninterrupted flow. If untoward events do occur, the whole process is started anew. If, for example, the actor stumbles or falls—that is to say, commits situational offenses—he will go back inside the house, sit down, drink some water, etc., pretending that there is no continuity between the earlier stumble and the new course of departure he or she is about to make. These actions of course take time as well, and a wholly new set of departure moves are initiated. The same is true if a person sneezes or hears a chirping gecko etc.; a new beginning is made and this time the ordering of events may turn out well. In the improbable event of it turning out bad again, the project may be abandoned for the time being.

However, once the initial stages of departures are completed, the second stage must be confronted. It is indeed a confrontation because this stage has to do with visual signs of fortune or misfortune. These omens are widely known by the members of the culture and are invoked in these ceremonies of departure. The omens are classified into two categories: seeing an item from one list is considered a "good" or "auspicious" omen, while an item from the other list portends "bad," "evil" and an inauspicious turn of events. (See Table 12.1.)

The visual and aural omens are easily classified into the two categories. The logic by which this is done is obvious: each item in

Table 12.1
Good and Evil Omens in Jaffna

Set	Good	Evil
Visual	Gold, diamond, holy beads; the color yellow, full pot, fruits, flowers, rice; milk, curd ghee, honey, sugar cane, toddy pot; grains, white costume, two or more Brahmins, king; virgin; wife; elephant; horse; bull; cow; monkey; deer; dog; peafowl; honey bee	Leather; charcoal, bones, wet mud; ashes, oil; firewood, cotton wood; iguana; cat; snake; rabbit; leopard; pig; bear; pigeon; the lame; mendicants; the ill; the shaven headed; those with hair undone; widows; barren women; enemies; hermaphrodites; dwarfs; those bearing arms; wet clothes; black and red flowers; clarified milk; empty vessels; smoke; fire
Aural	Holy songs; auspicious music	Wailing; sneezing; scolding; funeral drums
Move	From Right to Left: Eagle, owl, deer, dog, rat, mongoose, squirrel	From Left to Right: Eagle, owl, deer, dog, rat, mongoose, squirrel
	From Left to Right: Parrot, crane, peacock, hen, crow, buffalo, cat, spotter deer, fox, lizard	From Right to Left: Parrot, crane, peacock, hen, crow, buffalo, cat, spotter deer, fox, lizard

the evil category of visual omens is associated with death, either directly or indirectly. Indeed, they are all hot items connected to the very process of cremation. The good omens are cool, life-giving and auspicious. But this logic does not stand up for the movement-of-animal omens. The movement from right to left of one set of animals being auspicious while the movement of the same set of animals in the opposite direction being inauspicious is merely an arrangement in opposition deriving its meaning from being so classified: it is the movement from *right* that is auspicious just as it is the movement from *left* that is inauspicious. Another set of animals is used to establish a similar theme, though this time the relationship between leftward movement and inauspiciousness is reversed.

If any of the good items are encountered on first setting out on an important mission, the traveler immediately concludes that the auspices are good and the mission will succeed. Such a conclusion would be reached by the actors themselves and/or articulated by the others present in the occasion of departure. The actor, under these circumstances, then departs with greater confidence and diminished anxiety and uncertainty. Indeed, it can be presumed that such confidence and sense of well-being will have a commensurate effect on the person's subsequent performance which may well provide grounds for success and fulfillment.

In the event the actor encounters an ill omen, a number of options are available. If the contemplated mission is one of supreme importance, then it would be aborted and resumed later. If, however, the mission was of lesser importance, alternative steps would be taken to nullify the evil effects of a bad omen. For example, if the actor encounters a widow in white on setting out for a mission, he can always return, sit for awhile, and even ensure that the next outing is auspicious by placing a married women in a strategic place. Or the actor can go ahead and stop en route at a temple and make an offering (*puja*), thus nullifying the evil effects of the earlier encounter. It is indeed possible for the actors in such ceremonies of departure to stage the entire omen-situation so that only good ones are available. If, for example, a departure of momentous significance is about to occur, all inauspicious people (e.g., widows) would be subtly or not so subtly removed from the environment of the departure point just as all inauspicious objects (e.g., brooms) will be removed. In circumstances where such staging or restaging is not possible or is thought to be either too cumbersome or ineffective, steps are taken to nullify the portended ill-fortune. Whether good fortune is promised or not, the earlier encountered ill omen would become ineffective.

DRAMAS OF ARRIVAL

If departures are fraught with consequences, arrivals are pregnant with significance. In all societies, arrivals of relatives, friends, acquaintances, strangers, enemies etc., are treated differently by the receivers. It is the crucial moment in an encounter in which deference and demeanor establish the status, identity and mood of those who are arriving and those who are receiving. In the relations between nations, the arrivals and departures of the nation's representatives are stage-managed by hired hands to ensure that the proper deference and demeanor are maintained. The color of the carpet, the number of guns to be used in salute, and the status of the officials carrying out the reception-act are all important and encoded strictly to establish both uniformity and dependability. In the transactions of everyday life by less exalted people, the same properties obtain: the ceremonies of arrival indicate the status and identity of the actors, as well as establish the relative mood of the receivers at the arriver's arrival. In Tamil circles in northern Sri Lanka there are rituals of welcome for such arrivals, whether everyday or ceremonial. In the case of the former, the receiver of people who are of equal status or of higher status approaches the arriver and, with noticeable alterations in demeanor to indicate a smile, says "welcome" ("*Varungo*"), invites the arriver inside (if there is a room for such purposes), seats the guest and begins a conversation. A visitor who is of roughly equal status will be offered liquid refreshment. Such an offer and its acceptance complete the transaction. In fact, if the visitor begins to take leave before such an offer has been made, the host will say, "You are going without partaking of anything. Wait awhile: I will give you something to drink. . . ." It is more or less obligatory to accept the proferred drink at this stage. If the visitor is of a much higher caste than the host such an offer would not be made. If it *were* made, it would be done only tentatively and rejected on some excuse or other.

It is, however, only when kin or very close friends of the family arrive that the full structural implications of these rituals are made clear. They may of course come at any time, unannounced and unheralded. And when they do come they are treated with "proper respect" (*Mariyathai*). This indeed includes the ceremonies described earlier as well as the usual inquiries about health and happiness. However, if the guests have arrived on an *inauspicious* day, they will be denied any refreshment or sustenance from the household and will be told so. This is particularly the case with the first arrival after an important event like the New Year celebration or a marriage. The belief is that if the guests are entertained on an inauspicious day, they will never come again. Hence, if guests arrive on a day such as *Attami* (the eighth day after the new moon or full moon), they will be told not to wait for what may well be called any "alimentary communion." Such communion would of course complete the visit. The request will also signal the guests that they are such valued kin or friends that the hosts do not want to run the risk of losing them.

Certain days of the week and certain times within the day are set apart as auspicious ones. During these periods, believers seek to initiate enterprises. These designated times are based on the conjunctions of the planets and a firm belief in astrology. Certain conjunctions are said to be "good" and certain others are said to be "bad." In addition, certain of the good days are determined to be good for particular tasks: sowing, reaping, travelling, housewarming, getting married. Even more secure and particular relationships of an auspicious nature can be obtained for one's own horoscope. However, for marriages and for extraordinary arrivals (arriving for the first time in somebody's house, or returning after a long absence), the day and time will be considered.

[*Summary by A. Paul Hare:* Perinbanayagam reports that ritual and attitude in Jaffna, a community in Sri Lanka, are characterized by two ideas, "good" (life-giving) and "bad" (life-denial). Departures that are important to a person have to be staged. Should any bad omen be encountered (stumbling, sneezing, unwanted sounds) then the process must be started again. Having left the place of departure, the person must still be on the lookout for good or bad omens. If good omens are encountered, the actor departs with greater confidence that the mission will succeed. If bad omens appear, the mission may be aborted or the actor must do something to counter the omen.

Arrivals are also a matter of concern. The social status or kinship relationship of the visitor is important in determining the ceremony that will be performed. However, some times of day and year are auspicious and some inauspicious, according to conclusions based on astrology.

Perinbanayagam's account provides an example of social action that follows a "plot." There is a fairly explicit set of norms for the direction that the action should take and the behaviors that should be performed. However, some initiative is left to the actor, who must use judgement to decide which of the many possible variations should be enacted (see also Perinbanayagam, 1985).]

13

Funerals in America

Ronny E. Turner
and Charles Edgley

The study is based on unobtrusive observations of and information obtained from fifteen mortuaries in three cities. Funeral directors were interviewed, "in-house" manuals on how to successfully perform a funeral were subjected to content analysis, and both national and local advertising material were studied. Only funeral services performed in mortuary chapels (a growing trend) were studied; however, the techniques we describe are probably also applicable to services held in churches of various denominations. No memorial services in which the deceased had been cremated were included in our observations, and all of the funerals we observed were open-casket.

THE PERFORMATIVE NATURE OF FUNERAL DIRECTING

Funeral directors and allied members of their team may be seen as actors whose job it is to stage a performance in such a way so that the audience to it (the bereaved family and friends) will impute competence, sincerity, dignity, respect, and concern to their actions. Given the one-shot nature of the funeral service, and the

From "Death as theater: A dramaturgical analysis of the American funeral" by Ronny E. Turner and Charles Edgley, 1976, *Sociology and Social Research*, 60 (4), 377–92 (extract includes pp. 378–88). Reprinted [with minor agreed changes and with footnotes omitted] by permission.

impossibility of doing it over in the event of mistakes, funeral directors must necessarily be concerned with those performative aspects of their business which will lead the audience to be impressed favorably by their effective staging of the show. As in any other performance, the concern is likely to be with whether the show comes off or falls flat, and consequently, to use Goffman's phrase, the expressions given off must be arranged in such a way so that the images and impressions formed are favorable ones.

From the standpoint of the sociology of work, the funeral directors are in a unique business. They draw their living from a relatively fixed resource, the death rate in a community. They cannot increase the amount of business available to them by increasing the number of deaths in the community, and they must be very careful of how they advertise lest someone gain the impression that they want more people to die. (One does not, for example, see funeral homes sponsoring such risky events as the Indianapolis 500). Their choices for increasing the flow of money, then, are limited and center basically around two options: (1) Getting more than their share of the business from deaths that do occur in the community; and (2) merchandizing up, so that the average cost of a funeral rises. In short, their opportunities to make money stem from their performative ability to stage dramas which are meaningful to their audience, and will leave them with an impression favorable enough to contribute to the all-important "reputation" which funeral homes find is in many respects their most marketable, if not tangible, quality.

ROLE-DISTANCE: THE SACRED AND THE PROFANE

The performative necessities of their work are, however, made more difficult by another aspect of the relationship between the funeral directors and their audiences which has been pointed out repeatedly by various studies: the amount of social distance that exists both between them and their clients and between the object of their work (death), and the public they undertake to perform before. They deal with objects which are both sacred and profane; simultaneously loved and loathed. As a result, the funeral directors often attempt to separate the body work from the directive work, thereby putting distance between themselves and their traditionally assigned role. Sometimes this is accomplished in the same routine as when they dress out differently for embalming and for directing; at other times role-distance is accomplished by simply hiring separate functionaries to do the body work so that they can concentrate on staging the show without being seen as ... contaminated by contact with the dead. What is separated here by the funeral directors is not so much themselves from their role, but rather themselves from a loathsomeness ordinarily attributed to certain aspects of that role by their audience.

As in other occupations (the medical profession being the most salient example), some emotional detachment from the objects one is manipulating is desirable. Funeral directors and their staff, therefore, tend to separate their own personal identity from the task of embalming bodies. The language and non-verbal conduct in the preparation room, then, demonstrate a type of role distance which effectively communicates detachment and sometimes even disdainful alienation from the role one is performing.

BACKSTAGE REGIONS: PREPARATION AND REHEARSAL

A successful funeral is a sequence of activities performed by the funeral director and staff that are later seen by the bereaved as a respectful, appropriate tribute to the life and memory of the deceased. It requires an extensive series of preparations backstage, or behind the scene that will later be used for the performance. A backregion or backstage is simply the space for the enclosed activities strategically hidden from the audience. It is ordinarily a place, but it may also be constituted simply by the shielding and masking of information in an interpersonal situation so that the audience does not realize certain things which would conflict with the performance as staged. A backstage region, whether a place, or an interpersonal strategy is "bounded to some degree by barriers to perception."

The necessity of backregions is due, obviously, to the fact that preparations for performances, if seen, may contradict, alter, qualify, or destroy the impressions fostered frontstage. Because people seem to have a limited capacity for seeing ritual as ritual, and since funerals, like any other drama, are prepared for, the viewing of the preparations may undercut the impressions fostered frontstage. Similarly, those who have worked in the backregions of a restaurant, in the kitchen or afterhours, and have participated in the preparation of food, the classification of customers by the staff, and so forth, may have difficulty seeing the frontstage performances in the same manner again.

In the backstage, equipment and props used to produce the performance are stored, the behavior within the area is considered "private" and the scenes that go on are protected from public observance by various territorial imperatives socially constructed and enforced: doors, curtains, locks, and "employees only" signs.

THE BACKSTAGE SETTING

What we have said about backstage regions is generally applicable with few qualifications to the dramas of the American funeral. The preparation room, referred to by some morticians as a "medical laboratory" is spatially segregated from the funeral chapel, visitation rooms, viewing rooms, offices, and other regions the public frequents. It may be noted that the awesome and sacrosanct qualities of such places may be heightened by successfully identifying them with medicine, a line of endeavor which seems to establish particularly esoteric meanings for the bulk of Americans.

The social and physical boundaries that separate the preparation room from other parts of the home are essential to the ceremonial performances that will be given later. Here the corpse is washed, shaved, sprayed with disinfectant, sliced, pierced, creamed, powdered, waxed, stitched, painted, manicured, dressed, and positioned in a casket. Embalming involves the draining of blood via the major arteries while simultaneously refilling them through an injection point in the neck or armpit with fluid. Through the use of other chemicals the flesh is softened, stretched, shrunk, restored, colored, and even replaced.

Obviously, these procedures would be likely to shock "nonprofessionals" such as the friends and family of the deceased (Goffman, 1959:106). But more than that, such viewing would tend to present the audience with an impression that would contradict that being fostered frontstage. As Goffman notes, "if the bereaved are to be given the impression that the loved one is really in a deep and tranquil sleep, they will have to be kept away from the area where the corpse is drained, stuffed, and painted for its final performance." In the presence of family and friends the casketed body is never touched by mortuary personnel; they honor a distance of two to three feet from the body. However, the preparation room is characterized by handling of the body (a naked body in some procedures) in ways that would appear disrespectful and even inhuman, even if one were unaware of the identity of the deceased. One might respond to all of these by asking just how it is possible to talk about inhumanity when the object is a corpse, and yet it is precisely this "human identity" conception of the enterprise that supports the funeral profession, and indeed, becomes the basic polarity between which the morticians must balance their act. At any rate, the embalming, restoration, and other preparatory procedures requiring manual labor might appear to the lay person as morbidly intimate, repulsive, and a violation of dignity, even to the dead. Virtually all of the amenities persons accord to each other in everyday life are violated by the attendants who prepare a corpse for the service.

In order to maintain the historically hard-won image as a legitimate professional and counselor rather than an "undertaker" with all of its attendant morbid stereotypes, a funeral director must seclude the backstage by utilizing rhetoric less suggestive of what transpires behind closed doors. Here we come to the interpersonal shielding we discussed earlier which is at least as important as the barriers formed by physical space. It should be noted that backstage regions are protected not only by the funeral director, but also by others; most people, except some curious sociologists of everyday life, voluntarily avoid areas where they are uninvited. They exercise the sort of tact regarding settings that constitutes "discretion" (Goffman, 1959:229). In this sense, the audience actively, rather than passively, participates in the distinctions we have drawn. They want to be put on by the show as much as the producers of it, and they seem to recognize that part of the meaning of any performance will be diluted with disenchantment if one knows too much.

Even though the specifics of the preparation room are a mystery, most people know enough to choose acceptable ignorance and avoid trespassing into the region. Once again, the audience is a party to the stage production, avoiding asking questions about embalming procedures, and generally managing their behavior in such a way as to suggest they know nothing of such preparations, and want to keep it that way.

THE RHETORIC OF BACKSTAGE REGIONS

Both the technical and the informal nomenclature which mark the universe of discourse of backstage regions serve a number of functions, but they are sufficiently different from the language characterizing the frontstage production itself that they must be segregated from clients who seek funeral services. There exists quite clearly in the funeral business a backstage language and another rubric entirely for those occasions in which the performance that has been so laboriously prepared is being staged. A superb example of frontstage rhetoric is a sign on the door of the embalming room at one of the establishments we studied:

> REMEMBER
>
> This preparation room becomes sacred when a family entrusts us with one of its most precious possessions. Keep faith with *them* by conducting *yourself* as though the family were present. The body is dear to them. . . . Treat it reverently.

Backstage, however, morticians develop a very different set of behaviors toward their activities. Rather than being a person, the body becomes an object upon which one performs restorative art. And while the deceased is a dearly beloved, Mr. Doe, a father, a loved one, etc., during frontstage encounters with the bereaved family, backstage references are to various types of bodies such as "floaters" (one who has drowned and was not recovered until the body floated to the surface), "Mr. Crispy" (one who burned to death in an airplane crash), a "fresh" or "warm" one (a body received shortly after death), a "cold" one (a frozen body) [—such references] are encountered in the conversations of the backstage crew. References to restorative art in the information materials given the public may in fact be referred to in the preparation room as "pickling" or "curing a ham." The use of "bod" instead of "body," especially with younger female corpses, is not uncommon. Joking, singing, the discussion of political issues, and (infrequently) open sexual remarks, racial slurs, complaints about the size of some bodies, profanity, and other rhetoric inconsistent with the frontstage regions are employed as ways of distancing the embalmers from the role they are performing.

Similarly, frontstage references to the burial containers such as casket, gift to the deceased, home, place of rest, and so on, are referred backstage as coffins, stuffing boxes, tin cans, containers, stove pipes (a cheap metal over wood casket), or brand names given to caskets by manufacturers.

Such role-distance behavior may manifest alienation from the role "but the opposite can well be true: in some cases only those who feel secure in their attachment may be able to chance the expression of distance" (Goffman, 1959:128). Expression of distance may serve also to relax those attending the task and/or convey an atmosphere of "just another job" in what otherwise would be a situation permeated by anxiety and tension. As in other occupations, role-distance behavior can be noted in the many instances where the actor does "two things at once," singing, joking, and using the aforementioned backstage rhetoric while preparing the body.

The preparation room is a scene constructed in such a way as to establish the impression of a sterile medical atmosphere. Even though the backstage crew may humorously refer to themselves as a "bod squad," they more often refer to themselves and their behavior in medical rhetoric, thereby borrowing credence and legitimacy from that professional most esteemed in American society: the medical doctor. The medical atmosphere and terminology is also a part of on-going role-distance; the white surgical garb, the white walls, and the operating table help the practitioners to see and present themselves as at least quasi-medical professionals rather than simply handlers of corpses.

Just as theaters have their make-up rooms, the preparation room serves as a setting for the cosmetology that will turn the corpse into the star of the show. As make-up artists, morticians are unsurpassed, and have elevated their skill to a high art. Given the various causes of death and subsequent kinds of bodily disfigurement, "restorative art" is designed to make the deceased look natural and, in a sense, "alive." Cosmetics in the hands of a skilled mortician can cover a multitude of wounds, bruises, ravages of long-term disease and discoloration, and even major forms of disfigurement. (One funeral director told us with pride of a suicide he had reconstructed, even though the man had succeeded in blowing the top of his head off.) When successful, an unblemished star is born for a magnificent final performance.

As with other performers, the actor is not supposed to appear "made up," but rather the make-up is applied to convey "natural" impressions rather than the artificiality the make-up room as a backstage region implies. (One is reminded of the cosmetic company that advertises that women can achieve the "natural look" only by using their new line of cosmetics.) Funeral directors take as a compliment remarks that the deceased looked natural, at peace, younger than before, asleep, etc., apparently because their art is being validated by the very audience at which it is directed. What might be seen as "art for art's sake" is justified by funeral directors as a vital element in what has come to be known as "grief therapy," a vocabulary of motives (Mills, 1940) which most practitioners in the industry now espouse. Such a set of rationales hold that the viewing of the body by the bereaved is a necessary step in the acceptance of death. It is of interest to note that an economic vocabulary of motives might also apply (open casket funerals usually generate a larger expenditure of money because the interior designations of the casket become significant to the buyer), although it is, of course, never mentioned to the audience. Instead of such economic motives, the following rationale from a handbook on successful funeral practice is presented:

> Perhaps the most important function of the art of viewing the remains is the confrontation of the emotional fact that one is so anxious to deny. Seeing the dead body seems to break through the defenses more effectively and more completely than any other part of the funeral process (Raether, 1971:140).

FRONTSTAGE PERFORMANCES: BRINGING OFF THE SHOW

The change of titles from "undertaker" to "funeral director" has been perhaps the largest single clue to the dramaturgical functions the industry now sees itself as performing. They are indeed "directors," controlling a dramatic production. The staged performance is supported by elaborate backstage preparations of the body, equipment, and props, and the immediate family is rehearsed as to the schedule of events and protocol. In order to preclude any miscues in the performance, the rehearsal covers entrance cues, exit, places to sit, and timing of events; special requests by the family can also be included in the script and program.

The funeral directors and their crews continue backstage activities during the funeral service: automobile drivers, pallbearers, ministers, and musicians must all be orchestrated in a smooth and uninterrupted performance. As skilled directors, the morticians are available but largely unnoticed, particularly by the audiences of friends and acquaintances who come to pay their respects. They are often acutely sensitive to matters of "promptness, overall courtesy, ushering, and other tasks involving a sizeable number of people" (Raether, 1971:121). Their demeanor, of course, establishes a model of appropriate behavior in a funeral setting:

> The funeral director should not strut, nor should he appear to be mousey. His demeanor should show dignity, concern, and confidence ... [he] should not talk loud, nor should he whisper secretly. He should speak in a subdued voice ... should not walk around unnecessarily ... should not snap his fingers or hiss to get attention (Raether, 1971:121).

In addition, they constantly check the floral pieces for placement, fallen petals, water leakage, and all such tidying is made prior to the family's arrival.

CONTROLLING THE SITUATION: THE CAST OF CHARACTERS

The funeral as a staged performance features a marquee listing a well-respected director affiliated with National Funeral Directors Association; a star, the deceased, whose life and attributes comprise the plot; a supporting cast of the bereaved (one of whom usually takes charge of managing details); supporters of the bereaved; ministers; musicians; and pallbearers; and, of course, the audience of friends and acquaintances. The bereaved are themselves supporting actors and actresses, for they too are part of the performance.

They are "on-stage" in that their behavior is reviewed and judged by others whose comments on how well the family "held up" at the funeral will later be taken into account. Observations of funerals and especially post-funeral gatherings show that such evaluations comprise much of the conversation, and the bereaved who shows too little emotion for the audience's conception of their relationship to the deceased, or those who show too much when it is known that the relationship did not warrant it, are likely to be judged negatively. Mourners are aware of this, and may construct their performances accordingly. Sometimes, in fact, part of the directing task is coaching mourners on how to act.

Cast members must also be controlled: one of the most potentially troublesome of these is the minister. As such, he or she may, if not carefully managed, act in such a way as to construct a counterreality which can cast doubt on the entire show. Historically, the undertaker was a minor functionary whose role was under the direct supervision of the minister (Vernon, 1970:246–47); Habenstein and Lamers, 1955). However, with the emergence of the professional "funeral director" the ministers have been increasingly shunted to the background, and now it may be properly said that *they* are the minor functionaries. The counterreality that the ministers may establish is the idea that all of this funeral business is really nonsense because the body is a shell and the "soul" has departed. In addition, they may feel that there is too much emphasis on rituals involving the body, and that these smack of paganism and status seeking, as well as being a waste of money. The minister may have long years of close association with the family, and if allowed to operate unmanaged, can be a significantly moderating influence on the family's choice. Consequently, trade journals devote occasional space to giving helpful advice on how to control this potentially truculent member of the cast. *Mortuary Management*, for example, suggests the following when a minister comes with the family to make arrangements:

> We tell the family to go ahead and look over the caskets in the display room, and that the minister . . . will join them later. We tell the minister that we have something we would like to talk to him about privately, and we've found that if we have some questions to ask him, he seems to be flattered that his advice is being sought, and we can keep him in the private offices until the family has actually made its selection (Vernon, 1970:265).

THE FUNERAL HOME AS THEATER AND STAGE

Seldom are funeral homes space-age in architectural design; rather they present themselves with traditional white columns, Colonial style, or even proudly as older structures. They are usually decorated profusely with flowers, the walkways are carefully landscaped, the grass must be sprayed green during the winter months and of course the interiors are meticulously decorated. Such appearances are ways of establishing other meanings besides the usual ones of death and morbidity. Brightly colored drapes, curtains, and fixtures seem to breathe life; black hues are out, for they conspicuously betray the image of "undertaker." Even the traditional black limousine is no longer fashionable among more modern funeral homes; colors such as grey, white, and blue are now seen as more appropriate to death-free imagery.

The stage itself, the funeral chapel, is a model of theatrical perfection; many chapels would make a Broadway star envious. The chapel is usually arranged with ample entrances and exits, and may be served by back-doors, halls, tunnels, and passageways that lead from the preparation room without ever trespassing frontstage areas. Equipment and props such as flower holders, religious symbols and decorative roping are used to set the stage for the performance. In addition, the basic stage area is often neutral so that appropriate props can be used to establish the correct symbols for the various religious types of funerals common in our society.

If all of this background is successfully arranged, the funeral director—like other persons responsible for the direction of performances in our society—is in a position to control the kind of definitions that arise in the situation. Having had little opportunity to rehearse for such rituals, the majority of mourners face a highly problematic, tense, and relatively undefined situation. Consequently, monitoring the director's cues becomes a way of apprehending what the situation calls for.

Despite the best of scheduling, however, the inevitable "mistakes at work" occur. But while every funeral director can unreel a series of atrocity stories about things that go wrong, ordinarily the recovery techniques are successful in salvaging the show. Caskets are rarely dropped, leak, or have their contents spilled onto the floor, especially since the troublesome role of "pallbearer" has been successfully turned into an honorary position, with the actual carrying of the casket done by members of the staff. Expected contingencies such as "excessive" displays of grief are managed smoothly with cues being given to the clergy who may then minister to the person (Raether, 1971:21).

ESTABLISHING THE MOOD

A crucial, and therefore precarious feature of virtually all human affairs is mood. And it is important to remember that actions establish mood. The putting on of certain conduct will lead the reviewer to feel this way or that; and, as we have already shown, the review of the funeral directors' show is in many ways the most tangible product they sell.

Probably the single most effective way of establishing the right mood for a funeral is the judicious use of music. Emanating usually from a veiled location, "appropriate" organ music (as opposed to "inappropriate" music such as amplified guitar) is the vital medium through which the atmosphere of the funeral is created. In counsel with the family, the musical selections are planned to set the mood for serenity, beauty, respect, or whatever values are desired. Many mortuaries offer lists of musicians upon which the family can call, and who will perform for a fee; other establishments have their own musicians available for hire. As in other shows, the selection, volume, tone, and timing of the music provide cues for the series of events or acts that are presented. With the aid of a printed program, music cues the audience in sequence: be respectfully quiet; the service is beginning; the choir is about to sing; a prayer is forthcoming; a minister is about to speak; the eulogy is being delivered; it is time for the processional view of the deceased; the service is over—you may leave. Mood management, then, is a major means by which the director controls the situation.

FRONTSTAGE RHETORIC AND THE DENIAL OF DEATH

Although one of the consensually stated objectives of funerals is the acceptance of death by the family, the rhetoric of the frontstage as well as the social and physical setting of the funeral service itself tends to contradict such claims. Despite the many criticisms and subsequent industry denials and changes in procedure, the metaphors used in the American funeral continue to be those of sleep, transition to other worlds, and eternal life, rathe than death. Much of this denial, of course, stems from religious traditions which tend to treat death as a kind of minor nuisance on the way to glory. And there is little in the funeral to contradict such ideas. "Mr. Jones" reposes in a "Slumber room" in a casket whose mattress rivals the posturepedics designed for those of us still alive but suffering from back trouble. The titles and words of songs frequently sung at a funeral ("Death is only a Dream," "Asleep in Jesus," "It is not Death to Die") pointedly do not say "death has occurred, I am sorry" but rather "he or she is still with us."

In addition to this socially established denial of death, funerals serve as morality plays which weave social commentary into the ritual. Eulogies to the deceased will ordinarily contain references to their community service, character, righteousness, and approved identities. Certain behaviors are validated as noble, while others are by implication denounced. The audience is thereby advised to take note, for they too will someday be reviewed in such a public ceremony. One comforting aspect of such eulogizing, however, is that the deceased are usually given the benefit of the doubt; the eulogizer selectively parades their various careers. The dramaturgical necessity of such selectivity, of course, makes for considerable juggling of the available facts of a person's life, especially when dealing with those whose lives have been less than sterling. When mentioned at all, such elements will almost always be placed in contexts that were not used while he was alive: recalcitrance being redefined as "independence," or purposelessness as "a restless spirit," for example. Such rhetoric underscores Burke's (1935) contention that all dramas are essentially morality plays with the themes of deviance and respectability playing large parts.

[*Summary by A. Paul Hare:* Turner and Edgley share Goffman's interest in backstage activity and team performances as they describe the ways in which funeral directors in the United States manage their activity. The funeral directors need to separate two parts of their role that deal with sacred and profane aspects of their work. Body work is done backstage. When the director is working with relatives and friends of the deceased, the work is done frontstage. Each region has its own language and behavior. Manuals for funeral directors provide guidelines for appropriate action.

The funeral chapel is a model of a theatrical setting. There are many areas and devices for separating different types of activity and controlling the activity that does occur in each area.

As with the self-reconstitution rituals described by Sarbin, the theme at the funeral is often not a final death but a transition to another world or to eternal life. Like other rituals for birth, puberty, and marriage, the rituals associated with death provide a symbolic transition for the principal actor and also involve a change of status and new meaning for the roles of members of the family and others in the audience.]

Glossary

The meanings of some of the principal terms for dramaturgical analysis that we have introduced in Chapters 1 through 9 of this volume are presented below. We have not included terms introduced in the case studies of forms of enactment in Chapters 10 through 13.

achieved role: A set of expectations for a position that a person holds as a result of skill or knowledge or some other achievement.
act: Subdivision of a drama; might contain two or more scenes.
actable idea: an idea that provides a basis for individual or group action.
action area: the place where the central activity occurs; the action area includes both stage and backstage.
actor: a person who plays a part in a performance.
altercasting: the behavior of a person who induces others to play preferred auxiliary roles.
antagonist: an actor who represents an idea that opposes the idea of the protagonist, such as a villain.
ascribed role: a set of expectations for a position that a person is born into such as that based on gender or kinship.
audience: persons who observe a performance directly or whose opinions are important for the actors; an audience may include a part of the self, other actors, persons present who are not part of the performance, or reference groups.
auxiliary player: an actor supporting one of the principal actors (protagonists or antagonists).
avoidance processes: actions taken to avoid loss of face.
backstage: that part of the action area where actors prepare for their performances and special effects are produced.

backstage staff: persons who arrange the setting, provide costumes, props, and makeup for the actors, or take part in other activities that support the performance.

chorus: a set of auxiliary players who may serve to concentrate the spectators' emotions on particular themes and their attention on particular events.

comedy: a drama that has a good outcome which is attributed to a person or persons.

consensual reality: the validation for an enactment provided by an audience.

contextualism: a form of analysis of social interaction that places the emphasis on the "context" in which the action takes place; the root metaphor is the historical event.

continual observation: the method by which an audience contributes to the maintenance of role behavior over time.

corrective processes: actions taken to correct for an instance of loss of face.

cue: a discriminative response from an audience or from another actor that guides a performer.

definition of the situation: the meaning that the actors attach to the setting (including the presence or absence of others).

deroling: the process of moving out of one role before taking up another.

director: a person who provides an interpretation for the script, rehearses the actors, and provides cues at the time of the performance.

drama: the largest unit of dramaturgical analysis; includes the five phases of (1) developing an actable idea, (2) providing a stage, (3) selecting the actors and training them in their roles, and (4) enacting the idea, with the result of (5) new meanings for actors and audience.

dramatic situation: a set of roles representing a conflict between two directions of effort; a plot is composed of one or more dramatic situations.

embarrassment: a feeling that occurs when an individual does not do what ought to be done, given the social identities of the participants and the setting.

emotion: a transitory social role.

enactment: a phase of a performance, involving the acting out of one or more actable ideas.

episode: a dramatic performance, the natural unit of social activity.

face: reputation in the eyes of others.

face work: actions taken to make whatever a person is doing consistent with face; face work can involve avoidance and corrective processes.

farce: a drama that has a good outcome that is dominated by the situation.

fool: a comic role in a drama, with behavior that is usually upward (comparatively dominant), positive, and expressive.

frame: a definition of the situation, including an indication of the degree of seriousness or playfulness to be attached to an event.

hero: a protagonist in a drama whose behavior is usually upward (comparatively dominant), positive, and serious.

hungan: a person who specializes in becoming possessed by a god's presence.

I: the active part of the self.

illusion: a theatrical term for the process of confining attention to what is appropriate or meaningful or consequential for a defined level of reality.

image: an emotionally loaded set of words, physical object, or event that can become a focus of attention, especially in a small group.

individual perceptual field: a set of images in the mind of a group member.

interpersonal behavior: interaction between individuals, the observed behavior that results when the tendencies of a person's personality have been modified by the expectations of a role.

level of reality: definition of the situation, frame; three levels of reality are pretend (games, ceremonies), alternative (occupations, rituals), and overriding (efforts to change or defend the definition of the situation).

line: a definition of the situation sustained by a team.

Me: the inner audience, observing, encouraging, or restraining the actions of the "I."

melodrama: a drama that has a bad outcome attributed to the situation in which the actors find themselves.

monodrama: a type of self presentation in which an individual takes several parts by implying that several voices are speaking.

offstage: the areas where persons who support a performance, often at some distance from the stage (producers, directors, playwrights), do their work.

onlooker: the role of a person who collaborates in the unreality of a stage play as a member of the audience.

performance: an instance of social interaction, including a staged theatrical event, that progresses through five stages beginning with an idea and ending with new meanings for actors and audience.

personality: self, the individual behavior characteristics that a person brings to a role.

phase: a natural division of a drama.

playwright: the person who provides the original idea (image, theme, plot, or script) for a performance.

plot: a detailed scenario for action with an indication of the roles to be followed and the stages a group must go through to reach a goal, such as the guiding idea in a social movement.

pre-text: the written script for a drama.

protagonist: the actor who is the theme carrier of the moment, such as the hero.

psychodrama: a method of group therapy in which the director helps the individual who has a problem (the protagonist) explore the problem by enacting one or more scenes that represent aspects of the problem.

public drama: an occasion when the apparatus of the public media, official authorities, or professional practitioners act to build up a sense of an orderly world.

real: an instance of social interaction that has some actual function to perform.

reference group: a set of persons, real or imagined, who are important to an actor and whose opinions are used by the actor as a guide for performance.

role: a set of expectations for a part played in a performance; this text includes descriptions of two types of roles, dramaturgical (protagonist, director, audience, etc.) and societal (ascribed or achieved).

role conserve: a new understanding of a role that results from the enactment of a role.

role fatigue: the loss of energy available for a role because of continued unproductive role performance.

rounding: the moment when the quest of the shaman can go no further.

scene: a subdivision of an act, a self-contained sequence of events involving the same actors and the same action area.

scene/act ratio: the relationship between the setting and the performance; all aspects of the scene suggest limits for the action that will be appropriate in that setting.

script: a complete set of directions for social behavior, as in everyday routines or in manuals for organizations.

self: personality, the individual behavioral characteristics that a person brings to a role, including the capacity to distinguish one's self from others.

self reconstitution: a process by which an individual is brought to a new understanding of the self.

setting: stage set, which suggests a mode of appropriate activity.

shaman: a person who specializes in going into trance state to visit the place of the origin of creativity and understanding.

social interaction field: a dynamic entity that includes all the individual perceptual fields, plus the overt behavior by means of which individuals attempt to communicate to each other the content of their individual perceptual–evaluative fields.

social reinforcement: approval or dissapproval given to actors by an audience.

spontaneity/creativity: an adequate response to a new situation or a new response to an old situation.

stage: the part of the action area where the performance takes place in view of the audience.

symbolic: behavior of an actor that is intended to give meaning beyond that implicit in the actual behavior.

symbolic interaction: the "Chicago school" of social psychology that emphasizes the importance of the social construction of reality for understanding social behavior.

team: a set of actors who support a protagonist or who present a common front.

text: the actual staged performance of a drama.

theatergoer: the role of a person who carries out the activities necessary to attend a theatrical performance.

theme: a suggestion of movement over time, including both direction of movement, emotional tone, and a minimal set of roles, such as the guiding idea in an instance of collective behavior.

time line: a line divided into units of time with an indication of the limits of phases, acts, and scenes of a drama.

tragedy: a drama that has a bad outcome which is attributed to some person or persons.

villain: an antagonist in a drama who opposes the hero, and whose behavior is usually upward (comparatively dominant), negative, and serious.

warm-up: the first period of enacting a role in a group.

References

Abelson, Robert P. 1981. "Psychological status of the script concept." *American Psychologist* 36(7): 715–29.

Aguilar, John L. 1980. "Egalitarianism as dramaturgy: Ideology and social interaction in Mesoamerica." *Symbolic Interaction* 3(1): 105–21.

Allen, Vernon L., and Karl E. Scheibe (eds.). 1982. *The Social Context of Conduct: Psychological Writings of Theodore Sarbin.* New York: Praeger.

Bales, Robert F., and Stephen P. Cohen, with Stephen A. Williamson. 1979. *SYMLOG: A System for the Multiple Level Observation of Groups.* New York: Free Press.

Barbour, Alton, and Zerka T. Moreno. 1980. "Role fatigue." *Group Psychotherapy, Psychodrama and Sociometry* 33: 185–90.

Bentley, Eric. 1965. *The Life of the Drama.* London: Methuen.

Berger, Peter L., and Thomas Luckmann. 1967. *The Social Construction of Reality: A Treatise in the Sociology of Knowledge.* Garden City, NY: Doubleday.

Berne, Eric. 1964. *Games People Play: The Psychology of Human Relationships.* New York: Grove Press.

———. 1972. *What Do You Say after You Say Hello?* New York: Grove Press.

Brissett, Dennis, and Charles Edgley (eds.). 1975. *Life as Theater: A Dramaturgical Sourcebook.* Chicago: Aldine.

Buber, Martin, 1970. *I and Thou.* New York: Scribner.

Burke, Kenneth. 1935. *Permanence and Change: An Anatomy of Purpose.* New York: New Republic. (Second revised edition, 1954, Los Altos, CA: Hermes. Reprinted 1964. Also reprinted 1965, Indianapolis: Bobbs-Merrill.)

———. 1945. *A Grammar of Motives.* New York: Prentice-Hall.

———. 1968. "Dramatism." In D. L. Sills (ed.), *International Encyclopedia of the Social Sciences*, vol. 7, pp. 445–52. New York: Macmillan.

Burns, Elizabeth, 1972. *Theatricality: A Study of Convention in the Theatre and in Social Life*. New York: Harper Torchbooks.

Buss, Arnold H., and Stephen R. Briggs. 1984. "Drama and the self in social interaction." *Journal of Personality and Social Psychology* 47(6): 1310–24.

Cavan, Sherri, 1966. *Liquor License: An Ethnography of Bar Behavior*. Chicago: Aldine.

Caws, Peter. 1979. *Satre*. London: Routledge & Kegan Paul.

Cochran, Larry. 1986. *Portrait and Story: Dramaturgical Approaches to the Study of Persons*. New York: Greenwood Press.

Cohen, Abner. 1979. "Political symbolism." *Annual Review of Anthropology* 8: 87–113.

———. 1981. *The Politics of Elite Culture: Explorations in the Dramaturgy of Power in a Modern African Society*. Berkeley: University of California Press.

Cole, David. 1975. *The Theatrical Event: A Mythos, A Vocabulary, A Perspective*. Middletown, CT: Wesleyan University Press.

Combs, James E., and Michael W. Mansfield (eds.). 1976. *Drama in Life: The Uses of Communication in Society*. New York: Hastings House.

Cooley, Charles Horton. 1902. *Human Nature and the Social Order*. New York: Scribner.

Deegan, Mary Jo. 1978. "The social dramas of Erving Goffman and Victor Turner." *Humanity and Society* 2(1): 33–46.

——— and Michael Stein. 1978. "American drama and ritual: Nebraska football." *International Review of Sport Sociology* 13(3): 31–44.

De Man, Paul. 1984. "The epistemology of metaphor." In M. J. Shapiro (ed.), *Language and Politics*, pp. 195–214. Oxford: Basil Blackwell.

Denton, Trevor. 1970. "The presentation of self in household settings." *Anthropologica* 12(2): 221–40.

Dewey, Richard. 1969. "The theatrical analogy reconsidered." *American Sociologist* 4(4): 307–11.

Ditton, Jason (ed.). 1980. *The View from Goffman*. New York: St. Martin's Press.

Dotter, Daniel L. 1980. "The social construction of territory: Metaphor, self, and the meaning of space." *Sociological Forum* 3(Fall): 19–30.

Edelman, [Jacob] Murray. 1964. *The Symbolic Uses of Politics*. Urbana, IL: University of Illinois Press.

Edgley, Charles, and Ronny Turner. 1975. "Masks and social relations: An essay on the sources and assumptions of dramaturgical social psychology." *Humbolt Journal of Social Relations* 3(1): 4–12.

Effrat, Andrew. 1968. "Editor's introduction." *Sociological Inquiry* 38(2): 97–103.

Fry, Christopher, 1962. "Comedy." In S. Barnet, M. Berman, and W. Bruto (eds.), *Aspects of the Drama: A Handbook*, pp. 67–70. Boston: Little, Brown.

Gamson, William A. 1985. "Goffman's legacy to political sociology." *Theory and Society* 14(5): 605–22.

Geertz, Clifford. 1980. *Negara: The Theatre State in Nineteenth-Century Bali*. Princeton: Princeton University Press.

Gillespie, Joanna B. 1980. "The phenomenon of the public wife: An exercise in Goffman's impression management." *Symbolic Interaction* 3(2): 109–26.

Goffman, Erving, 1956. "Embarrassment and social organization." *American Journal of Sociology* 62(3): 264–71.

———. 1959. *The Presentation of Self in Everyday Life*. Garden City, NY: Doubleday.

———. 1961. *Encounters: Two Studies in the Sociology of Interaction*. Indianapolis: Bobbs-Merrill.

———. 1963. *Behavior in Public Places: Notes on the Social Organization of Gatherings*. New York: Free Press.

———. 1964. "The neglected situation." *American Anthropologist* 66(6, pt. 2): 133–36.

———. 1967. *Interaction Ritual: Essays on Face-to-Face Behavior*. Garden City, NY: Doubleday (Anchor Books).

———. 1968. *Asylums: Essays on the Social Situation of Mental Patients and Other Inmates*. Harmondsworth, England: Penguin Books.

———. 1970. *Strategic Interaction*. Oxford: Basil Blackwell.

———. 1972. *Relations in Public: Microstudies of the Public Order*. New York: Harper & Row.

———. 1974. *Frame Analysis: An Essay on the Organization of Experience*. New York: Harper and Row.

———. 1977. "The arrangement between the sexes." *Theory and Society* 4(3): 301–31. (Reprinted in M. J. Deegan and M. Hill, eds., *Women and Symbolic Interaction*. London: Allen and Unwin, in press for 1987.)

———. 1981. *Forms of Talk*. Oxford: Basil Blackwell.

Gross, Edward, and Gregory P. Stone. 1964. "Embarrassment and the analysis of role requirements." *American Journal of Sociology* 70(1): 1–15.

Gusfield, Joseph R. 1980. *Symbolic Crusade: Status Politics and the American Temperance Movement*. Westport, CN: Greenwood Press. (Reprint of 1963 edition, University of Illinois Press.)

———. 1981. *The Culture of Public Problems: Drinking-driving and the Symbolic Order*. Chicago: University of Chicago Press.

——— and Jerzy Michalowicz. 1984. "Secular symbolism: Studies of ritual, ceremony, and the symbolic order in modern life." *Annual Review of Sociology* 10: 417–35.

Haas, Jack, and William Shaffir. 1982. "Taking on the role of doctor: A dramaturgical analysis of professionalization." *Symbolic Interaction* 5(2): 187–203.

Habenstein, Robert W., and William M. Lamers. 1955. *The History of American Funeral Directing*. Milwaukee: Bulfin Printers.

Hamilton, Clayton. 1939. *The Theory of the Theater and Other Principles of Dramatic Criticism*. New York: Holt.

Hare, A. Paul. 1976. "A category system for dramaturgical analysis." *Group Psychotherapy, Psychodrama and Sociometry* 29: 1–14.

———. 1980. "A dramaturgical analysis of street demonstrations: Washington, D.C., 1971 and Cape Town, 1976." *Group Psychotherapy, Psychodrama and Sociometry* 33:92–120.

———. 1982. *Creativity in Small Groups*. Beverly Hills, CA: Sage.

——— (ed.). 1983. *The Struggle for Democracy in South Africa: Conflict and Conflict Resolution*. Cape Town: Centre for Intergroup Studies, University of Cape Town.

———. 1985. *Social Interaction as Drama: Applications from Conflict Resolution*. Beverly Hills, CA: Sage.

———, and David Naveh. 1986. "Conformity and creativity: Camp David, 1978." *Small Group Behavior* 17(3): 243–68.

Harré, Rom. 1979. *Social Being: A Theory for Social Psychology*. Oxford: Basil Blackwell.

———, David Clarke, and Nicola DeCarlo. 1985. *Motives and Mechanisms: An Introduction to the Psychology of Action*. London: Methuen.

———, and P. F. Secord. 1972. *The Explanation of Social Behaviour*. Oxford: Basil Blackwell.

Harrison, Paul M. 1977. "Toward a dramaturgical interpretation of religion." *Sociological Analysis* 38(4): 389–96.

Hopper, Marianne. 1981. "Five key concepts of the dramaturgical perspective." *Free Inquiry in Creative Sociology* 9(1): 47–52.

———. 1983. "Moral meaning in felony jury trials: A dramaturgical perspective." *Free Inquiry in Creative Sociology* 11(2): 189–97.

Hughes, Everett C. 1976. "The social drama of work." *Mid-American Review of Sociology* 1(1): 1–17.

Katovich, Michael A. 1984. "Symbolic interactionism and experimentation: The laboratory as a provocative stage." *Studies in Symbolic Interaction* 5: 49–67.

Keenan, Francis W. 1975. "The athletic contest as a 'tragic' form of art." *International Review of Sport Sociology* 10(1): 39–54.

Klapp, Orrin E. 1962. *Heroes, Villians, and Fools: The Changing American Character*. Englewood Cliffs, NJ: Prentice-Hall.

Ladlau, L. K. 1975. *The Cato Manor Riots*. Unpublished Master's Thesis, Department of History, University of Natal, South Africa.

Lahr, John, and Jonathan Price. 1973. *Life-Show: How to See Theater in Life and Life in Theater*. New York: Viking Press.

Levine, Ron H. 1977. "Why the ethogenic method and the dramaturgical perspective are incompatible." *Journal for the Theory of Social Behaviour* 7(2): 237–47.

Lewin, Kurt, 1935. *A Dynamic Theory of Pesonality: Selected Papers*. New York: McGraw-Hill. (Copyright 1935, published 1959.)

Lifton, Robert J. 1961. *Thought Reform and the Psychology of Totalism: A Study of "Brainwashing" in China*. New York: Norton.

Lipp, Wolfgang. 1984. "Kultur, dramatologisch." *Osterreichische Zeitschrift fur Soziologie* 9(1–2): 8–25.

Lofland, John. 1975. "Open and concealed dramaturgic strategies: The case of the State execution." *Urban Life* 4(3): 272–95.

Lyman, Stanford M., and Marvin B. Scott. 1970. *A Sociology of the Absurd*. New York: Appleton-Century-Crofts.

———, and Marvin B. Scott. 1975. *The Drama of Social Reality*. New York: Oxford University Press.

MacCannell, Dean. 1973. *Nonviolent Action as Theater: A Dramaturgical Analysis of 146 Demonstrations*. Haverford, PA: Haverford College, Nonviolent Action Research Project, Monograph No. 10.

McDougall, Joyce. 1985. *Theaters of the Mind: Illusion and Truth on the Psychoanalytic stage*. New York: Basic Books.

McLeod, John. 1984. "Group process as drama." *Small Group Behavior* 15(3): 319–32.

McPhail, Clark, and David Miller. 1973. "The assembling process: A theoretical and empirical examination." *American Sociological Review* 38(6): 721–35.

Mandler, Jean Matter. 1984. *Stories, Scripts, and Scenes: Aspects of Schema Theory*. Hillsdale, NJ: Lawrence Erlbaum.

Mangham, Iain L., and Michael A. Overington. 1982. "Performance and rehearsal: Social order and organizational life." *Symbolic Interaction* 5(2): 205–22.

Manning, Peter K. 1982. "Producing drama: Symbolic communication and the police." *Symbolic Interaction* 5(2): 223–41.

Marsh, Peter, Elisabeth Rosser, and Rom Harré. 1978. *The Rules of Disorder*. London: Routledge & Kegan Paul.

Mead, George H. 1934. *Mind, Self and Society.* Chicago: University of Chicago Press.

Meltzer, Bernard N., John W. Petras, and Larry Reynolds. 1975. *Symbolic Interactionism: Genesis, Varieties, and Criticism.* London: Routledge & Kegan Paul.

Merelman, Richard M. 1969. "The dramaturgy of politics." *Sociological Quarterly* 10(2): 216–41.

Messinger, Sheldon L., with Harold Sampson and Robert D. Towne. 1962. "Life as theater: Some notes on the dramaturgic approach to social reality." *Sociometry* 25(1): 98–110.

Miles-Brown, John. 1980. *Directing Drama.* London: Peter Owen.

Miller, Thomas G. 1984. "Goffman, social acting, and moral behavior." *Journal for the Theory of Social Behaviour* 14(2): 141–63.

Mills, C. Wright. 1940. "Situated actions and vocabularies of motive." *American Sociological Review* 5(6): 904–13.

Mitchell, Jack N. 1978. *Social Exchange, Dramaturgy and Ethnomethodology: Toward a Paradigmatic Synthesis.* New York: Elsevier.

Mixon, Don. 1983. "A theory of actors." *Journal for the Theory of Social Behaviour* 13(1): 97–110.

Moreno, Jacob L. 1953. *Who Shall Survive? Foundations of Sociometry, Group Psychotherapy, and Sociodrama* (Revised edition). Beacon, NY: Beacon House.

———. 1972. *Psychodrama,* vol. 1 (4th edition). Beacon, NY: Beacon House.

Morocco, Catherine Cobb. 1979. "The development and function of group metaphor." *Journal for the Theory of Social Behaviour* 9(1): 15–27.

Nelson, Katherine, and Susan Seidman. 1984. "Playing with scripts." In Inge Bretherton (ed.), *Symbolic Play: The Development of Social Understanding,* pp. 45–71. Orlando, FL: Academic Press.

Nieburg, H. L. 1981. "Theory-tales and paradigms." *The Journal of Mind and Behavior* 2(2): 179–93.

Overington, Michael A. 1977. "Kenneth Burke and the method of dramatism." *Theory and Society* 4(1): 131–56.

Perinbanayagam, R. S. 1974. "The definition of the situation: An analysis of the ethnomethodological and dramaturgical view." *The Sociological Quarterly* 15(4): 521–41.

———. 1981. "Dramas of structure, theory and performance in Northern Sri Lanka." *Anthropological Quarterly* 54(1): 36–43.

———. 1982a. "Dramas, metaphors, and structures." *Symbolic Interaction* 5(2): 259–76.

———. 1982b. *Karmic Theater: Self, Society, and Astrology in Jaffna.* Amherst: University of Massachusetts Press.

———. 1985. *Signifying Acts: Structure and Meaning in Everyday Life.* Carbondale: Southern Illinois University Press.

Polti, Georges. 1977. *The Thirty-Six Dramatic Situations.* Boston: Writer.

Porter, Dennis. 1977. "The perilous quest: Baseball as folk drama." *Critical Inquiry* 4(1): 143–57.

Raether, Howard C. 1971. *Successful Funeral Service Practice.* Englewood Cliffs, NJ: Prentice-Hall.

Raven, Bertram H., and Jeffrey Z. Rubin. 1983. *Social Psychology* (2d edition). New York: John Wiley.

Reeves, Richard Ambrose. 1960. *Shooting at Sharpeville: The Agony of South Africa.* London: Victor Gollancz.

Rosnow, Ralph L., and Marianthi Georgoudi (eds.). 1986. *Contextualism and Understanding in Behavioral Science.* New York: Praeger.

Rowan, John. 1983. "Person as group." In H. H. Blumberg, A. P. Hare, V. Kent, and M. Davies (eds.), *Small Groups and Social Interaction,* vol. 2, pp. 253–64. Chichester and New York: John Wiley.

Rubin, Jeffrey Z., and Nehemia Friedland. 1986. "Theater of terror." *Psychology Today* 20(3): 18–19, 22, 24, 26–28.

Sarbin, Theodore R. 1976 [© 1977]. "Contextualism: A world view for modern psychology." *Nebraska Symposium on Motivation* 24: 1–41.

———. 1984. "Role transition as social drama." In V. L. Allen and E. van de Vliert (eds.), *NATO Conference on Role Transitions,* pp. 21–37. New York: Plenum Press.

——— (ed.). 1986. *Narrative Psychology: The Storied Nature of Human Conduct.* New York: Praeger.

———, and Vernon L. Allen. 1968. "Role theory." In G. Lindzey and E. Aronson (eds.), *Handbook of Social Psychology,* vol. 1 (2d Ed.), pp. 488–567. Cambridge, MA: Addison-Wesley.

———, and Larry P. Nucci. 1973. "Self-reconstitution processes: A proposal for reorganizing the conduct of confirmed smokers." *Journal of Abnormal Psychology* 81(2): 182–95.

Schlenker, Barry R. 1980. *Impression Management: The Self-concept, Social Identity, and Interpersonal Relations.* Monterey, CA: Brooks/Cole.

Sharron, Avery. 1981. "Frame paralysis: When time stands still." *Social Research* 48(3): 500–20.

Snow, David A. 1979. "A dramaturgical analysis of movement accommodation: Building idiosyncrasy credit as a movement mobilization strategy." *Symbolic Interaction* 2(2): 23–44.

———, and Richard Machalek. 1984. "The sociology of conversion." *Annual Review of Sociology* 10: 167–90.

———, Louis A. Zurcher, and Robert Peters. 1981. "Victory celebrations as theater: A dramaturgical approach to crowd behavior." *Symbolic Interaction* 4(1): 21–42.

Sobel, Bernard (ed.). 1959. *The New Theatre Handbook and Digest of Plays.* New York: Crown.

Stebbins, Robert A. 1979. "Comic relief in everyday life: Dramaturgic observations on a function of humor." *Symbolic Interaction* 2(1): 95–104.

_______. 1986. "The definition of the situation: A review." In A. Furnham (ed.), *Social Behavior in Context*, pp. 134–54. Boston: Allyn and Bacon.

Steiner, Claude M. 1975. *Scripts People Live.* New York: Grove Press, Bantam Books.

Stone, Gregory P. 1982. "The play of little children." In C. Jenks (ed.), *The Sociology of Childhood*, pp. 195–204. London: Batsford.

_______, and Harvey A. Farberman (eds.). 1981. *Social Psychology through Symbolic Interaction* (2d edition). New York: John Wiley.

Stryker, Sheldon. 1981. "Symbolic interactionism: Themes and variations." In M. Rosenberg and R. H. Turner (eds.), *Social Psychology: Sociological Perspective*, pp. 3–29. New York: Basic Books.

Taylor, Irving A. 1975. "An emerging view of creative actions." In I. A. Taylor and J. W. Getzels (eds.), *Perspectives in Creativity*, pp. 297–325. Chicago: Aldine.

Turner, Ralph H., and Lewis M. Killian. 1972. *Collective Behavior* (2d edition). Englewood Cliffs, NJ: Prentice-Hall.

Turner, Ronny E., and Charles Edgley. 1976. "Death as theater: A dramaturgical analysis of the American funeral." *Sociology and Social Research* 60(4): 377–92.

Turner, Victor. 1974. *Dramas, Fields, and Metaphors: Symbolic Action in Human Society.* Ithaca: Cornell University Press.

_______. 1980. "Social dramas and stories about them." *Critical Inquiry* 7(1): 141–68.

_______ (ed.). 1982a. *Celebration: Studies in Festivity and Ritual.* Washington, D.C.: Smithsonian Institution Press.

_______. 1982b. *From Ritual to Theatre: The Human Seriousness of Play.* New York: Performing Arts Journal Publications.

_______. 1985. *On the Edge of the Bush: Anthropology as Experience.* Tucson: University of Arizona Press.

Van Laan, Thomas F. 1970. *The Idiom of Drama.* Ithaca: Cornell University Press.

Vernon, Glenn M. 1970. *Sociology of Death: An Analysis of Death-Related Behavior.* New York: Ronald Press.

Watson, Catherine M. 1982. "The presentation of self and the new institutional inmate: An analysis of prisoners' responses to assessment for release." *Symbolic Interction* 5(2): 243–57.

Watson, Jeanne, and Robert J. Potter. 1962. "An analytic unit for the study of interaction." *Human Relations*, 15(3): 245–64.

Weimann, Gabriel. 1983. "The theater of terror: Effects of press coverage." *Journal of Communication* 33: 38–45.

Weinstein, Eugene A., and Paul Deutschberger. 1963. "Some dimensions of altercasting." *Sociometry* 26(4): 454–66.

Wessels, P. J. 1960. Report of the Commission Appointed to Investigate and Report on the Occurences in the Districts of Vereeniging (Namely at Sharpeville Location and Evaton) and Vanderbijlpark, Province of the Transvaal, on the 21st of March, 1960. South Africa.

Wilkinson, Gregg S. 1974. "Psychiatric disorder dramaturgically considered." *The Sociological Quarterly* 15(1): 143–58.

Wilshire, Bruce. 1982a. *Role Playing and Identity: The Limits of Theatre as Metaphor*. Bloomington: Indiana University Press.

———. 1982b. "The dramaturgical model of behavior: Its strengths and weaknesses." *Symbolic Interaction* 5(2): 287–97.

Wright, Sam. 1978. *Crowds and Riots: A Study in Social Organization*. London: Sage.

Yablonsky, Lewis. 1953. "An operational theory of roles." *Sociometry* 16(4): 349–54.

Young, T. R., and Garth Massey. 1978. "The dramaturgical society: A macro-analytic approach to dramaturgical analysis." *Qualitative Sociology* 1(2): 78–98.

Zurcher, Louis A. 1982. "The staging of emotion: A dramaturgical analysis." *Symbolic Interaction* 5(1): 1–22.

Name Index

Subject Index

About the Authors

A. PAUL HARE is a Professor of Sociology at Ben-Gurion University of the Negev in Israel. He received a doctorate from the University of Chicago. His writing on social interaction in small groups includes *Small Groups*, co-edited with Borgatta and Bales, and the *Handbook of Small Group Research*. His work on *Creativity in Small Groups* and *Social Interaction as Drama: Applications from Conflict Resolution* provide the first outlines of the dramaturgical perspective that are elaborated in the present volume. He is also the author of many journal articles, the co-editor or editor of the volumes *South Africa, Cooperation in Education*, and *The Struggle for Democracy in South Africa*, and the founder and editor of the journal *Israel Social Science Research*.

HERBERT H. BLUMBERG lectures in psychology at the University of London Goldsmiths' College. He received a doctorate from the Johns Hopkins University and has authored or co-authored over thirty articles and chapters in social psychology and social research methods.

Paul Hare and Herbert Blumberg have collaborated in editing three volumes of case studies on nonviolent action: *Nonviolent Direct Action, Liberation Without Violence*, and *A Search for Peace and Justice*, and (together with Kent and Davies) the readings on *Small Groups and Social Interaction*.

Lightning Source UK Ltd.
Milton Keynes UK
19 January 2011

166022UK00005B/13/P

9 780275 927622